Training and Care of the Versatile Hunting Dog

BY

SIGBOT WINTERHELT

AND

EDWARD D. BAILEY

Published By
The North American Versatile Hunting Dog Association

No part of this book may be reproduced in any form without the written permission from the North American Versatile Hunting Dog Association.

Second Addition

This addition of the "The Training and Care of the Versatile Hunting Dog," has been edited by Roberta Applegate, under direction by and concurrence with The North American Versatile Hunting Dog Association's Board of Directors and the Executive Council.

Editor's Note

This year marks the 30th anniversary of publishing of "The Training and Care of the Versatile Hunting Dog." This manual, affectionately called the "Green Book" has been of incalculable value to The North American Versatile Hunting Dog Association and the novice and journeyman versatile dog owners for whom it was written. Words cannot adequately express the depth of gratitude felt by NAVHDA for the authors' work.

Since this book was first published, our knowledge of dog behavior and psychology has increased immensely. Consequently, training techniques and approaches have changed as well. As a consequence, some of the techniques and training aids commonly used in 1973 are no longer considered appropriate by knowledgeable dog trainers. A very few minor text changes have been made to reflect the modern, more informed techniques.

Good training!

North American Versatile Hunting Dog Assn.

For information contact:

NAVHDA
P.O. Box 520
Arlington Hts, IL 60006

Twelfth Printing

Copyright Office
Hull, Quebec
Serial Number 252644
Register 78
July 8, 1974
Copyright U.S.A. May 7, 1979

©2000 North American Versatile Hunting Dog Assoc.
(NAVHDA) TX 5-620-575

CONTENTS

INTRODUCTION   Page

    The History of the Versatile Hunting Dog — Purpose
of the Book — How to Use the Book   .   .   .   1

Chapter

1. Training for Behavior in the Home and
   Walking at Heel   4

2. Whoa and Come   10

3. Retrieving on Land   28

4. Retrieving from Water   55

5. Tracking   65

6. Sitting and Staying   71

7. Searching for Game   74

8. Pointing — Steady to Flush and Shot   .   .   .   78

9. The Down   89

10. Flushing on Command   96

11. Care of the Versatile Hunting Dog   98

12. Twelve Golden Rules for Training   103

ABOUT THE AUTHORS   104-105

INTRODUCTION

The History of the Versatile Hunting Dog

The European hunting breeds are often referred to as "all purpose" gun dogs, which is a literal translation of the German "All Gebrauchshund." We prefer to call these dogs versatile breeds, a name more suited to the dogs' true characteristics.

There are several breeds of versatile dogs common in continental Europe, and with four exceptions, all were developed during the last decades of the 19th century. The four exceptions are much older breeds and provided a base for some of the others. These four are the Weimaraner, the Vizsla, the Brittany Spaniel, and his German cousin, the Small Munsterlander Pointer. The most common versatile breeds may be divided into three groups: the shorthaired group (German Shorthaired Pointer, Weimaraner, Vizsla); the wirehaired group (German Roughhaired Pointer, German Wirehaired Pointer, Pudelpointer, Spinoni, Wirehaired Pointing Griffon); the longhaired group (Brittany Spaniel, German Longhaired Pointer, Large Munsterlander Pointer, Small Munsterlander Pointer).

The hound, bloodhound, pointer and waterpudel were the basic breeding stock most widely used to develop the short and wirehaired groups. The longhaired group evolved from the heidewachtel, waterpudel, and flat-coated retriever. Many breeders kept good records of their breeding programs, but others did not. Pedigrees as we know them were unknown in those days. Practical breeding experience, patience, and finally, a better understanding of genetic laws, established pure breeds.

Why Versatile Breeds?

In Feudal times, hunting was the exclusive privilege of the wealthy landowners. They held a monopoly on hunting for centuries and created a very cultivated sport, complete with strict dictates and customs. Their reputations and wealth demanded the very highest standards in everything associated with the hunt.

Each type of game called for dogs developed for that particular game. Large kennels were maintained with large staffs to handle and train the dogs. Many specialized hunting breeds still used today owe their existence to these men and the times.

The Industrial Revolution changed all this. New classes evolved in society. A greatly elevated standard of living created interest in many pursuits which before were restricted to the landed gentry. Hunting was one such pursuit.

Intense interest and the pressure of new wealth gave rise to new hunting laws which made the sport available to a much broader element of the populace. Most of these new hunters came from the middle classes — doctors, lawyers, judges, teachers, and all varieties of merchants and businessmen. They lived in cities and towns and had neither the space nor the time to maintain large kennels of specialized hunting dogs. This atmosphere opened the way for the idea of a versatile gun dog. Interest was enthusiastic and universal.

As hunting increased in popularity in the latter half of the 19th century, the need for a dog with more versatile characteristics became increasingly apparent. Using the existing breeds of hunting dogs, dedicated men set out to produce the various versatile breeds. Most of the breeds were produced at about the same time. There were some differences in physical characteristics, but the hunting characteristics were closely allied.

What were the breeders looking for and trying to develop? They wanted and got breeds that would handle a variety of game, both feather and fur, before and after the shot. The dogs had to possess a keen nose and strong pointing instinct, a lively temperament, eagerness to retrieve from both land and water, stamina, and a durable coat and hide that would not hamper the dogs' work in cold water. The dogs also had to be intelligent, relatively easily trained, and have a character compatible with living in or at their masters' dwellings.

PURPOSE OF THE BOOK

The original reasons for bringing the various versatile breeds to North America were probably as numerous as the numbers of dogs imported. Today the versatile breeds have a permanent niche with the hunting fraternity. As the areas of open hunting space decline and urbanization continues, hunters will more and more require one dog that can do an efficient job before and after the shot and on any game the hunter wants to bag.

Unfortunately, the versatile breeds have suffered from underuse of their potential for the most part. Primarily, their use has been as an upland bird dog capable of handling a variety of birds and limited use on waterfowl. Few have realized their full retrieving potential. Fewer still have been used as tracking dogs. They have been relegated to the "continental pointer" pigeon hole, a close working, methodical pointing dog for the on foot hunter. The other half of the versatile breeds' usefulness has remained dormant.

The main purpose of this book is to present training techniques and to teach how to use these techniques to enable you to have a truly versatile hunting companion. Obviously, these techniques are not the only correct ones. There are many innovations that lead to the same result — a completely trained versatile hunting dog. The basics presented here are not the begin all and end all. Individual cases need individual techniques. Hopefully the steps of training and the philosophy of training will enable you to innovate when the occasion demands.

A second purpose is to assemble and pass on information on the care you should give your versatile dog both at home and in the field. Any hunting companion responds better to training and works more efficiently in the field if he receives proper care, feeding, housing and grooming. A long and useful life depends on good care and training. Let down on one and you sacrifice the other.

How To Use This Book

This book is meant to train people to train their dogs. It is a textbook. There are no anecdotes, no tales of super feats by super dogs — none of the dogs pictured are champions. Most of the dogs are just honest hunting dogs or at least their owners are hopeful that they will develop into honest hunting dogs.

Before starting to train your dog, read through the entire book. Do not just grab up your dog and start training according to page 1 today and page 2 tomorrow. Many aspects of training go on simultaneously. The handler should know what lessons are to be given each day and should know what exercises should be brought together with other exercises and which ones should follow or precede others. We cannot emphasize too heavily — digest the entire book first, then begin to train your dog.

This book is not synchronized with the aging of a dog. It is arranged in chapters according to the various aspects of training. The chapter on training for "whoa" and "come" is followed by the chapter on training for retrieving. In actual practice neither follows the other, the training for both proceeds together. The two chapters should be used together. There are many other instances in this book where chapters will overlap in timing either in part or entirely. We ask that the book be used as a whole rather than adhering to the chapters separately and in the sequence in which they appear.

The training techniques described in this book might imply that they are only applicable to young dogs. Many people might have older dogs that need retraining or additional training. The techniques given can be used on older dogs as well as youngsters. However, older dogs might have developed bad habits, or might have learned only part of a given task. This makes the training more difficult, but not impossible. The handler must be more firm, more insistent on correct performance and more persistent in his efforts. Punishment for mistakes will have to be more harsh in many cases and praise less lavish in somes cases. But, with more firmness, the same sequences of lessons can be followed with completely satisfying results.

Chapter 1

TRAINING FOR BEHAVIOUR IN THE HOME AND FOR WALKING AT HEEL

The versatile dog was bred to be the hunter's companion both in the field and in the home. For this reason, the truely versatile hunting dog must learn to control his temperament from puppyhood onward in any situation and in any location. The dog must have good manners whether he is in the livingroom, the kennel run, the field or the marsh or walking downtown by his handler's knee.

EQUIPMENT REQUIRED (PICTURE 6):
1. Flat leather collar.
2. Chain choke collar or spiked choke collar.
3. Small chain 3 to 4 feet long with snaps at both ends.
4. Short leather leash.

STEP 1.

As soon as the puppy reaches 8 to 10 weeks of age he should wear a collar. At this stage, a leather collar of proper size is the best. After getting used to the collar for a few hours he should begin learning that he must be tied fast for short periods. The small chain with snaps on both ends is most practical for this.

A staple or screw eye is put into the floor or baseboard in the corner of the room where the dog is to have his future place in the house. Carry the pup to his corner and attach the chain to his collar and to the staple or screw eye. There probably will be quite a fight with most puppies at this stage but this should simply be ignored.

The pup should be watched carefully to ensure he does not become entangled badly or does not strangle himself with the chain or tangling the chain around legs of furniture. A chain choke collar should never be used, the leather collar is better. Also, the pup should never be tied up after feeding or after a strenuous playing session to avoid toilet accidents in the house.

As soon as the pup has stopped fighting and remains quiet, release him from the chain and put him back in his kennel or basement or room where he sleeps and is fed. After a few days of being tied in his corner for short intervals the pup gives up fighting and accepts the confinement. Never release the dog as long as he fights the chain, release him only after he has become quiet.

After the pup has accepted his confinement and no longer fights it, the handler can unhook the chain from the fastener and using the chain as a leash, coax the dog gently around the room. In a few days the pup accepts being led around in the house and outdoors. This becomes the first stage of walking at heel.

As the pup grows older, the duration of being restricted in his corner of the room can be extended. Later on the dog will stay at his place without the chain for as long as desired. More freedom of movement can then be allowed as the owner desires, but the corner will always be the dog's place whenever the owner wants the dog to be out of the way of activity or visitors.

The dog should never be allowed to bark or whine or be noisy in any way while on the chain except for the initial days when the pup is fighting it. The versatile dog must accept confinement from early life onward without complaining or being upset about it.

STEP 2.

The versatile dog must learn to pay close attention to the handler's knee and stay close to it when commanded to do so. He must learn to walk quietly on the leash through woods and around obstacles without tangling the leash and without constantly repeated commands. He should be able to move quietly and calmly beside the handler while stalking a pond to jump shoot waterfowl — moving when the handler moves and stopping when the handler stops. When commanded to walk at heel, the versatile dog should behave as though he was an extension of the handler's leg.

A spiked choke collar can be used to advantage in teaching the dog to walk at heel, if the dog is 8 months or older, but a chain choke collar can also be used especially on younger dogs. Attach the short leash to the choke ring. The dog should be on the handler's left side for right handed shooters, the reverse for left handed shooters. The first lessons should be inside, in a large room, garage or basement or in a fenced yard free of distractions. The dog is positioned standing to the left of the handler and with a wall or fence to the left of the dog so the dog cannot pull sideways, away from the handler. The left hand holds the leash so it is loosely attached to the dog to give it some play. At first the leash is used primarily as a guide for the dog. Only loosen the leash if the dog becomes overly frightened or frantic. Otherwise keep on walking. The right hand holds the leash tightly so the distance between the dog's collar and

Picture 1. Proper way to hold leash while walking dog at heel. Griffon. (Photo by Edward Bailey).

Picture 2. Proper way to walk at heel. Notice that training may progress year round, in winter as well as the warmer seasons. Griffon. (Photo by Edward Bailey).

Picture 3. Encourage dog to come along by slapping your leg and urging with your voice. Griffon. (Photo by Edward Bailey).

Picture 4. When dog attempts to pull ahead, a stride to the left, stepping on his toes teaches him to keep his mind on you. Griffon. (Photo by Edward Bailey).

the left hand is 12 to 16 inches so the dog cannot get behind nor pull ahead of the handler (picture 1 and 2).

The handler should encourage the dog by patting his thigh and saying "come" quietly and coaxing. When the dog is coming along willingly the command "heel", "by foot", "by knee", or even "walk" can be introduced. Which command is used is not important, one should be chosen and used exclusively and consistently. "Heel" is the most used in North America.

Command "heel" and walk slowly at first. If the dog hangs back, encourage him by slapping the thigh (picture 3). The wall or fence will prevent the dog from moving off to the side, a sharp tug on the leash particularly if a spiked collar is used will discourage the dog from pulling ahead. Proceed to the first corner and make a sharp right turn. Do not wait for the dog, the dog will hurry to catch up to the handler. Move away from the wall when the dog has made several right turns and is paying close attention. Cross the center of the room and make a left turn or two. If the dog tends to pull ahead when turning left, the handler can make a quick step sharply to the left so he steps on the dog's front feet (picture 4). After being stepped on a few times, the dog becomes more intent on watching for direction changes.

Change the speed of walking, even running or trotting. Also change the distance between turns, sometimes making one turn immediately after another, sometimes going 10 or 20 or 40 yards before turning. Alter the sequence of turns as well, so the dog does not anticipate a turn and to keep his concentration centered on the handler.

Picture 5.
Dog should learn to walk on same side of an obstacle as handler or he is brought up short by the spike collar or choke collar. Griffon.
(Photo by Edward Bailey).

STEP 3.

Once the dog has mastered walking at heel in a confined room or yard, the exercise can be altered by walking the dog past or around obstacles such as posts, boxes, chairs, trees or any obstacle. The dog must learn to walk on the same side of the obstacle as the handler or he is brought up short by the spiked collar or the choke collar (picture 5).

The exercises can now be conducted in the field or woods where strange scents and sounds will act as distractions. The dog must only pay attention to the handler and concentrate on staying close by the handler's knee. However, attention must be two directional in these exercises. The handler cannot let his attention wander from the dog or the dog will make mistakes, just as he will make mistakes if he stops concentrating on the handler.

In the confinement of the yard, the dog can also begin learning to walk at heel without the leash. First allow the leash to hang loosely when walking and making turns. When the dog is performing flawlessly on the loose leash, the leash can be removed and the dog commanded "heel" as the handler walks away. If the dog loses attention on the handler and starts wandering away, the leash is immediately put to use again. The dog should be praised and encouraged lavishly on any correct performance, but any disobedience must be immediately corrected. Correct heeling off leash depends much on the dog's temperament. The more desire a dog possesses the more often he will try to leave the side, and he will have to be corrected frequently.

No matter how well the dog learns to walk at heel off the leash, do not depend on his obedience alone in any potentially dangerous situation such as walking along a road where there is a chance of traffic passing. The best trained dog can have a lapse or a distraction that causes him to break. Should the dog suddenly dart onto a road after a squirrel or rabbit or some other dog, he can be hit by a passing car before the handler can stop him. The best policy is to always use the leash and not trust to training alone.

COMMON MISTAKES

1. The most common error is letting the dog learn he can pull and thereby lead the handler rather than being led by the handler. Generally, a dog that is unmanageable on the leash is hopeless when off it. The dog must learn the leash means completely under the control of the handler. The proper use of the spiked collar and stepping on the dog's front feet usually prevents the senseless pulling.

2. Another common mistake is failure to vary the speed of walking, the sequence of turns and location of the lessons. The dog must not be able to outguess or anticipate the handler.

3. Keeping the leash too short, the dog gets to pulling.

Picture 6. Upper left-choke collar; short leash; leather collar. Lower left-spiked collar 30 foot leash; whistle in center.   *(Photo by Edward Bailey)*

Chapter 2

WHOA AND COME

Training your versatile dog is like building a house. In each case the investment is a long term one, but more important, each must have a solid foundation. The foundation on which all further training rests is the command "Whoa". Most of the control depends on "Whoa" and control, in the broad sense, is the whole of training.

Training a dog to "whoa" can be done in the house, in any room, a basement or in a fenced yard. The important thing is to have a minimum of distractions for the dog during the lessons until both dog and handler are ready for distractions.

EQUIPMENT REQUIRED (PICTURE 6):
1. Training Table (Diagram 1, page 27).
2. Short Leash 6 feet flat leather.
3. Long Leash 30 feet flat webbing.
4. Chain Choke Collar.
5. Whistle.

STEP 1.

Attach short leash to inner ring (the sliding ring) of choke collar. This gives the handler the most direct contact with the dog and does not allow lag between handler's signal tug and dog's receiving. Move collar up on neck so it is pressing into the back end of the dog's jaw bones (picture 7).

STEP 2.

Lead dog up ramp, over table and down other side several times. Now, lead the dog up the ramp onto the table. Command "whoa" as soon as the dog is on the table, forcibly stop him and make him stand.

Picture 7. Correct attachment of leash and use of collar. Pudelpointer. (Photo by Vern Brand).

10

This step is sometimes very difficult, but it is a very important step. Many dogs fight with determination, either actively or passively, to resist being led onto the table. No matter what antics the dog goes through, he must go onto

The following series of 5 pictures illustrate a dog fighting the table the first time he is led onto it. The 5 pictures were taken over a period of ten minutes. The fifth picture shows the dog accepting the table, and the first basic steps of whoa.

Picture 8. Dog fighting table first time up. Griffon. (Photo by Joan Bailey).

Picture 9. Dog still resists, but not as actively. (Photo by Joan Bailey).

Picture 10. Dog still resisting, but gaining some confidence from handler. (Photo by Joan Bailey).

Picture 11. Dog begins to relax. (Photo by Joan Bailey).

Picture 12. The dog has accepted the table and is well along in the first steps of whoa. The handler must persevere, no matter how determinedly the dog might fight the table. Note eye to eye contact. (Photo by Joan Bailey).

the table. You are not hurting him even though he may yelp or cry or even stand on his head or roll on his back. Even the most difficult dog will gradually become progressively easier to lead onto the table (pictures 8 to 12). Some dogs offer no resistance and clamber up like they have done it a hundred times before.

Should the dog fight extremely hard to avoid being led onto the table, he must be forced on, first from one end and led off, then from the other. This should be repeated, changing direction frequently, until he accepts going onto the table without fighting. Then begin with the first "whoa" command.

Once on the table and stopped by the "whoa", the dog must remain motionless — completely motionless. This is not to be expected immediately. However, this is where the table aids the trainer. The dog is up off the ground on what he considers an unstable support and on an unfamiliar surface. He is used to the ground and can afford to defy you more there. Also, the unfamiliar table top helps focus his attention on the trainer. The physical elevation of the dog on the table places the trainer closer to the dog's level and so less intimidating to the dog. From the trainer's side, the table saves a great amount of bending and in this stage of training a lot of hand to dog contact is required.

When stopped on the table, the dog must be made to stand erect. If the dog has not been taught to sit previously, this task is made less difficult. Prevent sitting by lifting the dog's back end with one hand placed between the back legs. Hold the head up and still by lifting the leash so the collar puts slight pressure on the jaw bones and throat (Picture 13) or the tension on the leash can be relaxed and the right hand can be used to hold the head erect by applying the pressure with the thumb and middle finger on the base of the jaw bones. *Do not* lift a dog by the tail. A dog's tail is extremely sensitive. It is an organ of communication *from* the dog, not *to* the dog and should not be used as a handle.

Each time the dog attempts to move he must be told "Whoa" and replaced in precisely the same spot. If only one foot is moved, it must be put back with the repeated "Whoa". Repetition of the command cannot be overdone. The more it is repeated, the stronger the dog will associate the command with being motionless.

The continuous repetition — whoa — whoa — whoa — whoa in a *quiet* voice while stroking the whole length of the dog's back and gently stroking the underside of the tail helps relax the dog while driving the command firmly home. The word "whoa" should be drawn out — wh-o-a soothingly, and softly. Always use the same soft and soothing expression on the word whoa. Later, when the dog is pointing game, the same command given in the same way will be used to calm and soothe the dog. Only when the dog is disobedient or stubborn should the whoa be given sharply and with a slightly raised inflexion in the voice. There is no need to raise your voice to a yell. Whenever you yell at your dog it says you have lost control, both of your dog and yourself. If this should happen, first control yourself, then back up in your training progress to something the

Picture 13. Prevent dog from sitting by lifting the dog's back end with one hand placed between the back legs. Vizsla. (Photo by Vern Brand).

Picture 14. With the leash slack but still held by the handler, the handler walks all around the dog — front, sides and finally behind. Any move by the dog must be corrected immediately. Vizsla. (Photo by Joan Bailey).

dog can do. When the dog performs correctly, praise him and quit for the time being.

At this stage in the training the dog is building confidence in and respect for the trainer. The trainer must cultivate this confidence and respect in order to bring out the dog's innate desire to please. The success of future training and field performance depend on it. A dog with little or no desire to please his master can and usually does become an uncontrollable self hunter and will be worse than useless in the field.

When the dog relaxes to the point where he will remain motionless with the pressure slackened on the collar and under his hind legs, he can be released from the "Whoa".

STEP 3.

Give the command "Come" *followed* by a tug on the leash and lead the dog down the ramp and trot him around on the ground before leading him back onto the table for a repeat of the lesson. Never give the command to come *after* the tug. The spoken command releases the dog from the "Whoa", not the tugging on the leash. Soon the tug will not be necessary.

Every command has also a releasing command. "Whoa" means stop and remain still no matter what or how long and do not move until a releasing command is given. "Come" is one of the commands the dog will learn as a release command that means "come to me" or "come with me". Later the dog will learn other commands that will also release it from "Whoa", such as a command to resume hunting, to retrieve or to go in a new direction or at a different distance or speed.

STEP 4.

Repeat as in Step 2, but on this and future repetitions of Step 2 gradually increase the possible things that will cause the dog to move or make him think he can move from the "Whoa" without the release command. Initially, keeping hold of the end of the short leash, back away from the dog, then walk around in front, to the sides and finally behind (Picture 14). Whenever he moves correct him with "Whoa" and replace him in the exact position.

Tug on the leash to pull the dog forward but do not command "Come", keep repeating "Whoa". The dog should resist the pressure in his attempt to obey the "Whoa" (Picture 15 and 16). Always correct immediately if the dog moves. As soon as the dog performs correctly on any of the attempts to tease him into mistakes, he can be told "Come" and led from the table. Do not let training lessons become boring for the dog. Whenever a lesson is done correctly, be satisfied with progress, no matter how small. Always end the training session with the dog doing something correct. Never end on a mistake or with the trainer going away mad.

There can be no set duration of a lesson. How long a lesson should be is dependent upon the dog's attention span. Some days the attention span can be nothing at all, other days it might extend to 20 minutes or longer. A very young dog 2 or 3 months old will have a shorter span than a dog 6 months old generally, but this by no means holds for every case on every day. Short duration lessons of 10 to 15 minutes given 2 or 3 times a day is much more successful than a 1 hour attempt every second or third day. The lessons must be short enough to keep the dog from being bored and frequent enough to keep the dog from forgetting what he learned the previous lesson. Unfortunately, there is no rule for striking this happy medium. The trainer must simply feel his way with each individual dog and in each particular situation.

The learning process that takes a dog from untrained to trained is not a straight smooth line. Expect many flat places in the climb, even some places that go down hill a bit. But, if you keep working correctly with the dog, the line will start to climb again. In the end, the general trend will be upward despite the flat places.

STEP 5.

Repeat Step 4 using the long leash so you can move farther from the dog but still keep leash contact. Keep tempting the dog into mistakes. Only through correction of mistakes can the dog learn what not to do.

STEP 6.

Repeat Step 4. By now the dog should be well versed in "Whoa" with the leash held. Lead the dog onto the table using the short leash. Command "Whoa". When the dog has relaxed, release the leash and walk around the

Picture 15. While repeating the command "whoa" the handler tugs on the leash. The dog should resist the pressure in his attempt to obey the "whoa". Weimaraner. (Photo by Vern Brand).

Picture 16. The tugging pressure is increased by the handler and the dog resists the pressure correctly. Weimaraner. (Photo by Vern Brand).

table. If the dog moves, go to him and correct him. Keep repeating until the dog will remain motionless for up to several minutes while he can see you. When the dog remains whoaed while you walk away some distance you can progress to stepping from his sight such as around a corner of a building, behind a tree and so on. Or, go into another room if training the dog indoors. Always return to the dog to release him from whoa. Do not command come until you have returned right to the dog. At this stage the dog should not yet be given the opportunity to get out from under your complete control, and the dog learns you will return to him. Also, never command the dog to come if you are standing behind him. Always face each other before commanding "come".

STEP 7.

Repeat all the previous steps but now on the ground without the use of the table. This sometimes is a very difficult transition to make because the dog is on his familiar home territory. Also, the dog might have associated trotting around between bouts on the table with the release from whoa. For these reasons, the trainer must start again with step 1 and proceed through the steps. After the initial resistance, most dogs fall quickly into the routine and progress through the steps is rapid.

Picture 17. To overcome tendency of dog trying to sit or lie down, loop free end of leash under dog's belly in front of hind legs and up about 2 feet to form handle with center of leash. Brittany Spaniel. (Photo by Vern Brand).

If the dog resists by trying to sit or lie down, the trainer can overcome the tendency by looping the free end of the leash under the dog's belly just in front of the hind legs. Run the free end of the leash up about 2 feet. By holding the end and center of the leash in one hand above the dog, you form a handle much like on a suitcase and you can forcibly keep the dog from sitting or rolling over without constantly bending down to lift him (Picture 17). At times it might be necessary to lift the dog's rear end either using the toe of your foot under and between his hind legs or bending and lifting with your free hand.

Again, on the ground as on the table, continuous repetition of the whoa is a must. Release the dog from "whoa" with "come" as previously described. Keep changing the location of the lessons to various places in your yard or house so the dog begins to learn "whoa" is to be obeyed anywhere and anytime. However, with "whoa" as with any command you ever give your dog, do not give the command unless you can enforce it at the moment you give it.

As with the lessons on the table, the dog should be repeatedly challenged and teased to try to induce him to move from whoa. Tug on the leash, push him, run around him, create distractions, even throw things like a glove or hat.

All dogs love to run through an open door ahead of the handler. The handler can utilize this trait to advantage to tease the dog into a mistake and teach him to control his eagerness. Lead the dog to a closed door — preferably one that swings away from the dog and handler. Command "whoa", then slowly open the door while cautioning the dog with repeated drawn out "whoa". Open the door fully and step slowly through the doorway. Keep a close eye on the dog all the time and be ready to quickly pull the door shut. Return slowly to the dog, praise him, then command "come" and lead him through. If the dog should attempt to move through the doorway before the command is given, close the door fast, so it hits the dog. This lesson quickly and strongly convinces the dog that when under the command "whoa", he must not move until told to do so by the release command "come".

STEP 8.

Once the dog has learned to remain motionless both on leash and when leash is lying loose, give the command "whoa" while leading the dog first on the short leash then on the long leash. Do this while you are walking and while running with the dog. When the "whoa" is given, the handler should also stop. Later the handler can run with the dog, command "whoa", drop the leash and keep on running. The dog should stop and remain where whoaed even if the handler runs 50 yards beyond the dog.

STEP 9.

Most people prefer to handle their dog with a whistle. Though not absolutely necessary and sometimes even a hindrance, the whistle is useful for handling your dog at a distance. The sound is sharper and carries farther and clearer than voice, especially in the presence of other noise such as leaves rustling, corn stalks rattling and so on.

The whistle commands can be added to voice commands at any time during the preceding steps. All the training can be done with whistle alone if desired. However, the trained dog should know both voice and whistle because there are times when hunting when you want to whisper a command to your dog such as in a duck blind or when stalking waterfowl in a pond or slough. In these situations a blast on a whistle would be inappropriate, besides spoiling your hunting.

Adding whistle commands to voice commands is a matter of the dog making the association between whistle and voice. To accomplish this, lead the dog onto the table, blow one blast on the whistle followed immediately by the spoken "whoa" which he should already know and being responding to. After a few repetitions the whistle sound alone will be sufficient. However, keep using both the single blast and spoken "whoa" interchangeably until the dog responds equally and perfectly to either or both.

Similarly, add 2 short tweet-tweet whistle sounds to "come". The 2 short sounds followed by the spoken "come", followed by the tug on the leash will gradually have the dog generalizing to the whistle calls.

STEP 10.

Continue to whoa the dog first on the table and then on the ground. But, now when the dog is whoaed on the ground remove the leash, walk away a short distance — 10-12 feet. Command "come" with voice or whistle. If the dog comes immediately, praise him, attach the leash and lead him away. At this time the handler can perform Step 8 again before repeating Step 10 with increased distance.

However, the dog is free in this step and might choose to run or wander away. If he does, repeat Step 5 with the long leash a few times. When he performs perfectly on the long leash, unhook the snap from the collar and lay it either loosely over the dog's neck or at his feet. Back off 10-12 feet but keep the leash in your hand so there still appears to be a line from you to the dog. Command the dog to come. If all previous steps have been followed, the dog will come on command, the tug long since having become unnecessary. The dog, under the impression he is still on the leash, should come to you with no problem. The leash should be hauled in and snapped to the collar when you "whoa" the dog by your side and the lesson can be repeated or Step 8 can be performed.

The distance between handler and dog should be changed often during this lesson. Also, the time between stopping and giving the command should be varied. The dog must not be allowed to learn that when the handler stops he is to come or to anticipate the command in any way. Only the command "come" releases the dog from the "whoa". No matter how far or how long or how many times the handler stops or what the handler does, the dog remains on whoa until commanded otherwise.

Step 11.

After the dog has thoroughly learned and completely understands that he must remain on the precise spot where he was whoaed, and when he comes directly to the handler when commanded, the handler can teach the incoming dog to stop on command.

Command "whoa" and walk away from the dog to a distance of about 30 feet. Keep watching the dog all the time to be sure he does not move. Wait a few moments, then command "come". When the dog is coming toward you, take a few steps toward the dog commanding "whoa". Walk to him when he is stopped and praise him, but keep him whoaed. Walk away again and repeat the lesson from a slightly different distance and angle.

If the dog does not perform the exercise correctly, do the whole exercise with the dog on the long leash. A caution on this exercise is needed. *Do not* overdo this lesson with a dog that shows tendencies toward softness or shyness. With such a dog, this exercise can result in the dog coming slowly or hesitantly toward the handler.

When the dog has reached these later stages in the whoa training, it is essential to keep varying the steps and the situations. Only when the dog immediately obeys "whoa" under any and all circumstances can you say your dog is trained to whoa on command.

Step 12.

The final test of the dog on whoa is to have the dog running freely 50 yards or farther from you and to stop on a single command—voice or whistle — and remain motionless until told to move. But, if the dog has progressed through all the steps, the transition is not too great. The foundation was laid in Steps 8, 10, and 11 when the dog has been carefully schooled on the long leash and remains when the handler runs on. Repeat the same format without leash and with distance between handler and dog gradually increased on each repetition starting just a few feet from the dog. The dog realizing it is free might try to ignore the command. For this reason the dog should be looking at the handler and the handler looking at the dog. From all the previous lessons the dog should already become familiar with the eye to eye contact almost as well as leash contact.

The first few lessons in this step where the dog is off the leash should be given in an enclosed, fenced-in area such as a school yard, fenced backyard or similar place. The area should be large enough to accommodate the exercise, but not so large that the dog does not realize he is confined. The dog, feeling confined, will obey the "whoa" more readily.

How many times the lesson should be given in a fenced in area before going to an open area depends on the temperament of the dog and on the intensity and completeness of the training he has received. A bidable, eager to please dog might progress quickly while a more high strung, independent dog would take longer.

The harder to handle dog can be brought under control easily. Put a fairly wide leather collar on the dog. Put one front foot of the dog through the collar up past the first joint, so the dog's foot is dangling in front of the collar. The dog must now run on three legs. He can be caught easily if he attempts to run away and, being partly disabled he is much more prone to obey. After about 20 minutes the legs should be switched to keep the dog from becoming over tired on one leg. Though this measure might sound drastic, it does not hurt the dog. After only a few lessons the dog should be under control and obeying the "whoa" when off leash and the tying up of one leg can be discontinued.

STEP 13.

When the dog has learned to remain still wherever whoaed in the presence of distractions such as the handler making noises, throwing objects, running toward and away from the dog and so on, the dog can be introduced to live game as a distraction. The purpose of this step is to lay the groundwork for making the dog steady when game is flushed in front of him.

Up to this point, the dog should *absolutely not* be given any command if he flushes and chases game. If the dog has been taken out for exercise and has found game prior to this point in his training, the handler should bite down hard on his tongue and keep his mouth shut like no other time in the life of the dog. No command is more wasted than yelling "whoa" at an unprepared dog when he is chasing game. And, no command has been misused more in such situations than the command "whoa".

This step is included in the "whoa" sequence in order to make the work of steadying the dog on game in the field easier. To prepare the situation — or set the stage — put a staple or ring in the ceiling above one end of the table top. Attach a piece of string such as fishing line about 20 feet long to a small net such as the netting on a landing net. Place a quail, pigeon, chukar partridge or similar bird in the net and tie net so bird has freedom to move around and flutter. Run the free end of the string through the staple (or ring) and hoist the net containing the bird up to the ceiling. Secure the end of the string to hold the bird up. Obviously, do not allow the dog to watch the procedure.

Bring the dog on the long leash, lead him onto the table and "whoa" him near the end opposite from where the bird is. Cautioning the dog with the drawn out "whoa", slowly lower the bird in the net until it rests on the table top 3 to 4 feet in front of the dog (picture 18).

Picture 18. This exercise can be done outside as well as inside a building. The staple or ring can be put almost anywhere and the training table carried to wherever you find a convenient area. In this picture the handler has an assistant to raise and lower the quail. Griffon. (Photo by Joan Bailey).

The movements of the bird in the net will get the dog very excited and he might attempt to lunge at the bird. The handler must prevent this with a sharper "whoa" and a quick pull on the leash (picture 19). If the dog freezes onto a sight point, the handler should cautiously and soothingly "whoa" him. After a few lessons, the dog will know he is expected to remain steady. The trainer can then move around the dog, behind him or to the front (picture 20). Tugging on the string will cause the bird to move or flutter and further entice the dog. Repeated quiet "whoas" will calm the dog and keep him still. The handler can even make the bird swing pendulum-like in front of the dog.

* * *

The importance of whoa cannot be overemphasized. It is the one command that means stop whatever you are doing and be still. It means do not chase, hold still while I cut your nails or remove a thorn; it means be still and quiet in a duck blind, stay here til I return for you; it means stop and find out what direction I want you to go; it means do not chew the leg off the chair or stay on that mat until your feet are dry. Whoa is the one word that means control of your dog in all conditions.

Picture 19. If the dog gets very excited and attempts to lunge at the bird, the handler must prevent this with a sharp "whoa" and a quick pull on the leash. Griffon. (Photo by Vern Brand).

Picture 20. After a few lessons, the dog will know he is expected to remain steady. The trainer can then move around the dog, repeating quiet "whoas" to calm the dog. Pudelpointer. (Photo by Vern Brand).

How many sessions or how long a period is required to reach the complete training on "whoa" cannot be stated precisely. Some individuals can advance through all the steps in a week; others might go on for 2 or 3 weeks; some up to 2 months. The dog's temperament, the trainer's temperament, conditions during any given lesson, accidental set backs, age of the dog, and many other variables all act to determine how long.

In actual fact, practice in whoa and reinforcement of the command continue throughout the dog's life. However, the progress through the training steps should be according to the pace set by the dog. Most dogs will be able to master all the steps in 2 to 3 weeks with 1 or 2 short lessons each day. If your dog takes longer, do not become overly worried. Individual dogs differ widely in maturation rates, cooperativeness and many other factors, so unequal rates of progress should be expected.

The important features to remember are: proceed one step at a time, go to the next step only when the preceding step is mastered, constant repetition of the command you are trying to teach, praise for your dog when he performs correctly and quick correction when he makes a mistake, demand complete obedience and attention from your dog in all training sessions, do not give a command you cannot immediately enforce.

The lessons in whoa can begin when a dog is 3 to 4 months old, though 5 to 6 months is better for most dogs. Remember, very young dogs 3 to 4 months old have a very short attention span, they are just starting to develope social relationships with people and they are not yet fully physically developed. For these reasons the lessons with young dogs should be short and with not too much pressure. There is no maximum age at which to start, but dogs who have already formed habits will be more difficult.

SUMMARY OF THE WHOA SEQUENCE:
1. Whoa on the table.
2. Come — the release from whoa.
3. Whoa with distractions and relaxed leash.
4. Whoa with long leash.
5. Whoa on the ground.
6. Remaining still for extended time.
7. Whoa and come without leash.
8. Whoa at a distance when dog is free.

COMMON MISTAKES TO AVOID DURING THE "WHOA" TRAINING:
1. One common mistake is too much use of a loud voice during the early stages of training. The trainer must prevent the dog from getting accustomed to a loud sharp command. The louder, sharper "whoa" must be saved for those occasions when the dog is disobedient or particularly stubborn. The trainer should learn from the beginning to draw out the word "wh...o...a" and to use the sharper "whoa" when it is necessary.

2. A common mistake is made in the lessons when the dog is learning to remain stationary while the handler walks away. The handler should keep his eyes on the dog constantly, which means backing away, ready to detect any attempt the dog makes to move. The attempt to move must be anticipated and corrected before the dog actually moves by raising the voice when commanding "whoa".

3. Another mistake often made when the handler walks away from the stationary dog is the handler always walks to the same place, stops and immediately calls the dog either on or off the leash. The dog soon makes the association between handler stopping and the immediately following "come" and begins to come as soon as the handler stops, not waiting for the spoken or whistled command. To avoid this, the handler should walk away from the dog, stop, wait a few seconds, move again, stop, wait, walk a few steps toward the dog, then stop and command "come" by voice or whistle, whichever the dog is accustomed to. The young dog should learn as early as possible that he must wait patiently and relaxed until the sound of the command signal for "come" permits him to leave his spot.

4. A common mistake is attempting to rush through the lessons and starting work off the leash too soon. The first time the command "whoa" is given to the dog when off the leash or outside an enclosed area, the handler must be sure his dog will obey. In many cases the young dog has not learned the basics of obedience well enough before being asked to whoa at a distance. This pushes the dog into being disobedient. The same applies for the mistake of trying to "whoa" a young dog in the presence of game in the field when the dog is not yet able to control his drive to chase in the face of such a tempting influence. Too often we find the young dog whose training has been too superficial, on the receiving end of an electronic training device designed to solve all problems and bring instant obedience. There is no substitute for step by step sequentially taught obedience that has been so well drilled that it is second nature to the dog. An electronic shocker collar used by the right hands at exactly the right moment can be an aid in training a problem dog. But, in the hands of the novice such a device is like the straight razor in the hands of a monkey.

5. Once the dog has learned to whoa correctly at any distance, the command should be used wisely and in accord with the temperament, aggressiveness to find game and the ability of the dog. Dogs that tend to be very dependent on the handler and are slow to develop an independence in searching for game should definitely not be whoaed while they are searching. Such dogs can easily become overtrained.

As with the young dog that has not yet mastered the "whoa" command completely, the overly dependent dog should only be commanded "whoa" when coming in toward the handler or when coming up to a road or fence.

The command should never be given when the dog is going out to search for game. This is not meant to push the dog over the farthest horizon, but rather to encourage him in searching. The dog that checks back to his handler too frequently and is fearful of going more than a few yards from the handler can benefit by being whoaed when coming in if the handler then walks up to the standing dog and when reaching him sends him in an outgoing direction. This use of whoa encourages the dog and gives him more confidence.

Instructions for Building Training Table

The table is 8' x 2' and about 2' high with a ramp on each end. The easiest way to build the table is from one sheet of plywood 4' x 8' x ½ or ¾ inches. Cut the sheet in half the long way. Cut one of the halves in half the short way. This gives a total of 3 pieces — one 2' x 8', two 2' x 4'. Fasten one of the 2' x 4' pieces to each end of the 2' x 8' piece with hinges so they can be folded flat over it and serve as the ramps. Nail some strips across each of the ramps to help the dog's traction. Put some 2' long legs under it and a bit of bracing. The legs can be made to fold to provide easy storage and hauling.

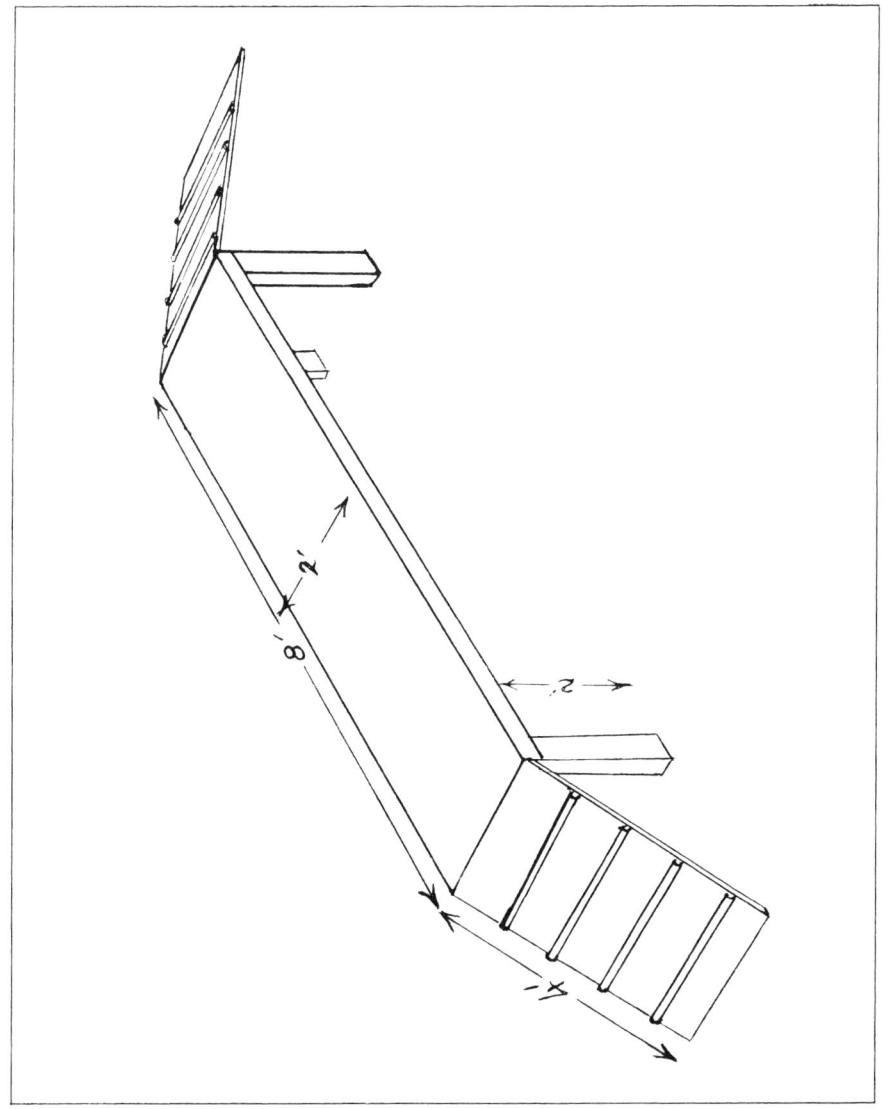

Diagram 1. Training Table.

Chapter 3

RETRIEVING ON LAND

The retrieve, like the whoa is based on two commands. "Whoa" stops the dog and holds him still, "come" releases him from whoa. Similarly, "fetch" tells the dog to go out, search for and find something, pick it up and return to the handler. "Out" releases the dog from the retrieve and means open your mouth and give me what you retrieved.

All retrieving training for all dogs should be force training. This word force does not mean abuse the dog in any way. Force training means a force of will, not punishment. It means proceeding one step at a time from the most elementary to the finished product. It means the dog retrieves whatever you want it to retrieve because it was commanded to do so. A dog that retrieves because it likes to carry things or because it is a game of fun will at sometime let you down. When a dog that retrieves because he feels like it does let you down, you have no recourse but to retrieve the game yourself. And if you have any respect for the game you are hunting, you will retrieve it even though you might have to wade a ditch of chest deep icy water to do it. What could be worse than to watch a duck you have crippled fall on an island 50 yards out and when the dog swims to the island and finds the duck, he refuses to pick it up and return. There is no way to get it because your dog doesn't feel like making the retrieve and you cannot convince your dog that you want him to bring it back on his return swim.

Force training is the only way to get consistent retrieving performance. And, it is the only way that gives the trainer the right to tell the dog to fetch with the certain knowledge that the dog will obey.

Picture 21. Dummies for retrieving training. Top left — light weight dummy equipped with chin strap. Top right — weighted dummy with weights that can be added. Bottom — bird wing. (Photo by Vern Brand).

EQUIPMENT REQUIRED:
1. Training Table.
2. Short leash 6 feet flat leather.
3. Long leash 30 feet flat webbing.
4. Chain choke collar.
5. Whistle.
6. Light dummy equipped with chin strap.
7. Weighted dummy to which more weights can be added.

STEP 1.

Retrieving training can begin as soon as the dog's permanent teeth have replaced the puppy teeth. Retrieving lessons go on at the same time as lessons in whoa and come and proceed simultaneously and in conjunction with them. After only a few sessions with "whoa" on the table, the dog will stand with the leash hanging loosely. At this time the retrieving training can begin.

Whoa the dog on the training table and drop the leash. If right handed, stand facing the side of the dog so his head is toward your right shoulder, his tail toward your left. (If left handed, the reverse would be more comfortable for the handler). With the left hand over the dog's muzzle, force the dog's mouth open by squeezing his left upper lip against his teeth with your fingers and his right upper lip with your thumb. Give the command "fetch" in a firm but quiet tone of voice at the same time pushing the light weight dummy into the dog's mouth. (picture 22).

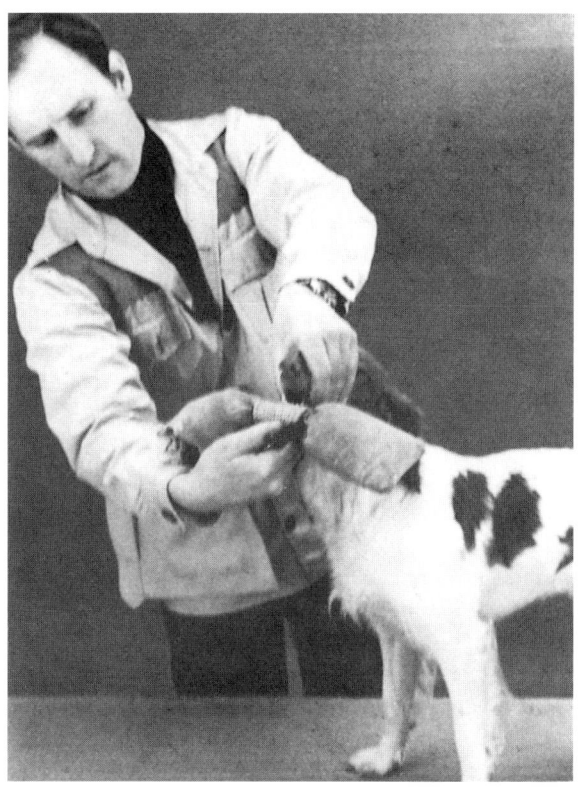

Picture 22. With the left hand over the dog's muzzle, force the dog's mouth open by squeezing his left upper lip against his teeth with your fingers and his right upper lip with your thumb. Give the command "fetch" in a firm but quiet tone of voice at the same time pushing the light weight dummy into the dog's mouth. Brittany Spaniel. (Photo by Vern Brand).

Be very sure the dog's lips are not caught between its teeth and the dummy (Picture 23). The dummy should be centered in the dog's mouth and placed just behind the canine teeth (fang teeth). Keep repeating the command "fetch" over and over again.

Most dogs will resist violently when the dummy is placed in the mouth. They will try to push it out with their tongue, paw with the front feet, attempt to spit it out or shake it out. Some will collapse, roll over, try to jump from the table or do anything to get the dummy out of the mouth (pictures 24-28). The dog must learn from the very first that he

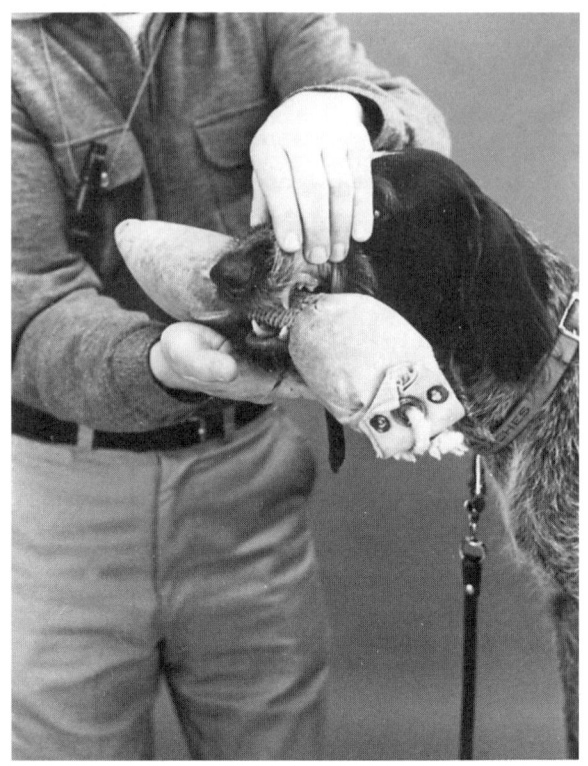

Picture 23. Be sure the lips are not caught between the dog's teeth and the dummy. Lift the lips with your fingers on each side to be certain. German Wirehaired Pointer. (Photo by Vern Brand).

must hold it and never release it until you give the command "out". The dog must be prevented from getting rid of the dummy. To accomplish this, the trainer keeps his left hand on the back of the dog's head and neck while holding the collar firmly. The right hand is held under the lower jaw holding the dog's mouth shut and keeping the dummy in place (picture 29). Never attempt at this stage to hold upper and lower jaw together either with one or both hands. This will make the dog fight even more. The middle finger of the right hand should be pressed firmly between the lower jaw bones so the trainer can feel the movements of the dog's tongue (picture 30). The instant the dog relaxes and stops fighting the dummy, command "out" and take the dummy from the dog's mouth. Now praise the dog by patting and stroking and telling him "good dog". Do not use the dog's name when praising him at any point in the lessons. The dog's name means the same as come or attention to the dog and so should be avoided for preventing confusion.

The dog might sit down during the initial lesson while fighting to avoid the dummy. This can be allowed at this stage. Later, the dog will not fight the dummy and will remain standing.

Picture 24. Handler has just placed dummy in dog's mouth. Griffon. (Photo by Joan Bailey).

Picture 25. Dog then begins to fight the dummy in an effort to get it out of his mouth. Griffon. (Photo by Joan Bailey).

Picture 26. Dog continues to fight, but handler keeps his left hand holding collar at back of dog's neck and head, right hand held under the lower jaw, preventing dog from spitting out the dummy. Griffon. (Photo by Joan Bailey).

Picture 27. Some dogs also try to dislodge the dummy by using their front feet. Handler prevents this tactic same as above. Griffon. (Photo by Joan Bailey).

Picture 28. A few minutes later the dog has realized that he cannot dislodge the dummy from his mouth, and he has accepted it. The handler can let go of the collar and praise and calm the dog with his hand and voice. Griffon. (Photo by Joan Bailey).

Picture 29. The dog must learn from the very first that he must hold the dummy and never release it until you give the command "out". The trainer keeps his left hand on the back of the dog's head and neck while holding the collar firmly. The right hand is held under the lower jaw. Griffon. (Photo by Vern Brand).

Picture 30. The right hand is held under the lower jaw holding the dog's mouth shut and keeping the dummy in place. The middle finger of the right hand should be pressed firmly between the lower jaw bones so the trainer can feel the movements of the dog's tongue. The instant the dog relaxes and stops fighting the dummy, command "out" and take the dummy from the dog's mouth. Praise the dog by patting and stroking and telling him "good dog". Griffon. (Photo by Joan Bailey).

Picture 31. When the trainer feels that the dog is relaxing and holding the dummy he can relax the pressure under the dog's chin by removing his hand and holding it about 12 inches from the dummy, all the time repeating the command "fetch", "fetch", "fetch". German Shorthaired Pointer. (Photo by Vern Brand).

This lesson can be repeated immediately or repetition can be interspersed with steps in "whoa" and "come". Changing from a fetch-out lesson to a whoa-come lesson and back to a fetch-out lesson or two helps keep the lessons from becoming boring to the dog. And, many dogs will be more relaxed in the "whoa" while they are holding the dummy.

STEP 2.

When Step 1 ceases to be a big struggle and the dog relaxes while holding the dummy for 15 or 20 seconds before you command "out", some teasing can begin. The clever dog will quickly associate the hand reaching for the dummy and the command "out". Soon he will anticipate the command and drop it as soon as the hand moves. This is a mistake that must be corrected immediately or better still, avoided. Be sure to praise the dog lavishly when he holds the dummy and scold him immediately when he drops it before the command is given. Softly spoken praise for correct performance relaxes both the dog and the trainer.

As soon as the dog holds the dummy and allows the trainer to relax the pressure under the dog's chin (picture 31) the handler makes false reaches for the dummy, touches the dummy, taps it with the finger tips and grasps it while repeating "fetch" (picture 32). Then give the "out" and take the dummy from the dog (picture 33). Do not overdo the teasing. At first a tap or two on the dummy will suffice. The purpose of tapping the dummy is to simulate objects bumping the bird as the dog retrieves in the field later on and to try to induce a mistake which can be corrected. The teasing is an essential aspect of the training, not a circus trick and must be done with purpose in mind.

Should the dog attempt to drop the dummy, he must be stopped and forced to hold it while a stern "fetch" is commanded. When the dog is again relaxed and holding the dummy firmly, try it again. But never let the dog get rid of the dummy until you command "out".

STEP 3.

Until now, the handler has been forcing the dog's mouth open and placing the dummy. Now the dog must learn to open his mouth and grasp the dummy himself when given the "fetch" command. Some dogs will do this quite readily, but most need more drastic measures. Remember, the dog must retrieve because the handler commands it, not just because it likes to or feels like it. So, do not feel over confident to the point of laxness if your dog appears to be a natural retriever.

A moderate method will work for some dogs. Rest the dummy well back on the heel of your right hand, keeping the hand flat. Touch the finger tips to the dog's chin, raise the heel of your hand so the dummy rolls or slides toward your fingertips and the dog's mouth. Simultaneously with raising the heel of your hand give the command "fetch". Your left hand should be holding the dog and keeping the dog's head in position so he cannot turn away (picture 34). The dummy bumping the front of the dog's mouth and the firm "fetch" can be enough to induce the dog to open his mouth and grasp the dummy.

A more harsh but eventually more certain method is to pinch the dog's ear while commanding fetch. While holding the collar with the left hand, grasp the dog's ear between the left thumb and forefinger. Hold the dummy in the right hand just in front of the dog's mouth, command "fetch" and apply pressure with your left thumbnail (picture 35). The instant the dog opens his mouth, usually to yelp, quickly place the dummy in the mouth and simultaneously release the pressure on the ear. The dog must associate grasping the dummy and the stopping of the pain. Usually this association is made very quickly.

Picture 32. To prevent the dog from dropping the dummy before the command "out" is given, tap the dummy with your finger tips, make false reaches for it, all the time repeating "fetch". Pudelpointer. (Photo by Edward Bailey).

Picture 33. (below) After tapping and reaching for the dummy several times, command "out" and take the dummy from the dog. Pudelpointer. (Photo by Edward Bailey).

Many dogs will try to snap at the hand that is pinching the ear. This must be stopped immediately because the dog must learn that the only way to stop the pain of the pinching is to open his mouth to receive the dummy and no other way will stop the pain. If the dog tries to snap, a sudden slap on the side of the muzzle with the hand that is pinching the ear — not with the dummy or the hand holding the dummy — delivered the instant the dog turns its head will usually suffice. Make the dog hold the dummy for a few seconds, command "out" and take the dummy from his mouth. Lavish praise on the dog, pat him, but keep him whoaed. The lesson can be repeated immediately or interspersed with "come", leading him from the table and again repeating the whoa lesson or another fetch lesson.

Picture 34. Roll the dummy into the dog's mouth as you give the command "fetch". Brittany Spaniel. (Photo by Vern Brand).

Now is also the time to get the dog used to holding various light weight things other than the dummy. Items like hardwood dumbbell shaped objects, bird wings, rolled up fur such as a rabbit skin and all sorts of light weight objects should be employed so the dog learns that anything must be held in his mouth until commanded "out".

STEP 4.

When the dog has progressed through Step 3 to the point where he is opening his mouth to receive the dummy without the ear pinch, he must be made to reach for it. At first an inch or two is adequate. Hold the dummy in

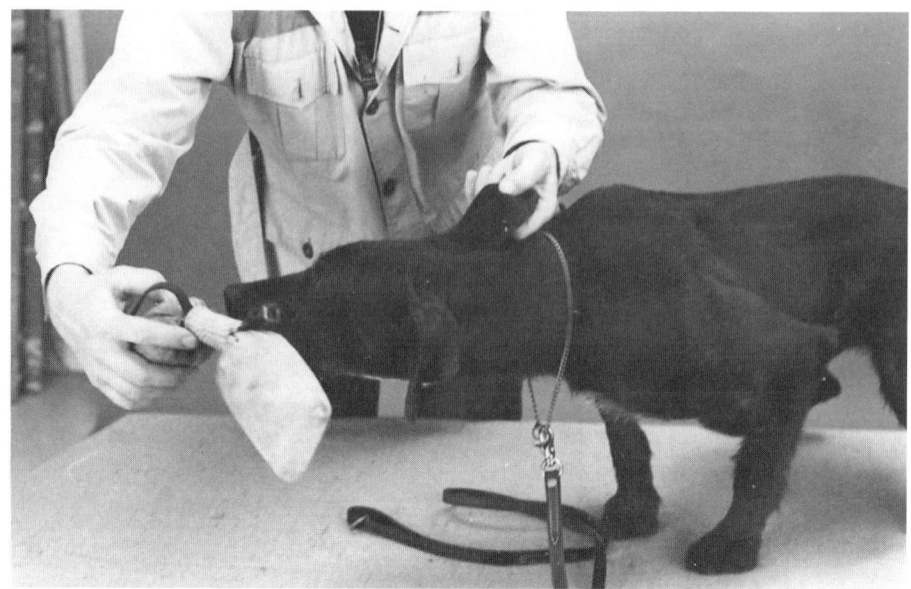

Picture 35. To teach the dog to grasp the dummy himself, hold the dog's ear between the left thumb and forefinger, while holding the collar with the same hand. Hold the dummy in your right hand, just in front of the dog's mouth, command "fetch" and apply pressure with your left thumbnail. The instant the dog opens his mouth, quickly place the dummy in the mouth and release the pressure on the ear. Pudelpointer. (Photo by Vern Brand).

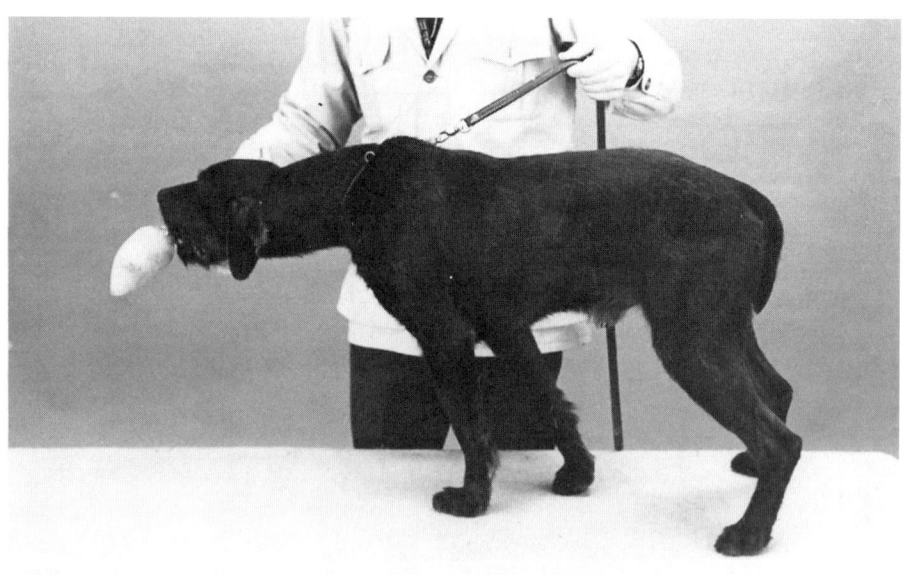

Picture 36. To get the dog to reach for the dummy, hold it in front of his mouth, command "fetch". Pudelpointer. (Photo by Vern Brand).

front of his mouth, command "fetch". If he does not immediately reach for it, pinch the ear (picture 36). He will quickly learn what he must do to stop the pain. As soon as the dog reaches to grasp the dummy, the pinching must stop. Allow the dog to hold the dummy for several seconds, tease him by tapping the dummy, command "out" and again praise lavishly. Be sure always that the "out" command is given before taking the dummy.

Gradually hold the dummy farther away and lower, changing the distance by only a few inches each time. Eventually the dummy will be resting on the table in front of the dog's front feet. Keep the hand on the dummy and command "fetch." The dog should not need to move his feet to pick up the dummy at this point. He is still under the "whoa" command.

Step 5.

This step in the training is often the most difficult to accomplish. The dog must now learn to pick up the dummy when the trainer's hand is not touching it. Always until now, the trainer held the dummy and the hand was the guiding influence. Without the hand on the dummy the dog loses his best visual cue. This tends to disorient the dog and confuse him.

To overcome this difficulty the trainer's hand is still necessary to keep the dog oriented. First have the dummy resting on the table with the fingers of the right hand touching it. Then, after several successful pick ups, just the forefinger touching (picture 37) the dummy. Gradually the pointing finger can be moved away from the dummy, an inch or so at a time until it no longer is needed as a direction signal. If any time the handler sees the dog is hesitant or confused during the withdrawal of the pointing finger, the trainer should retrace the progression, putting the finger closer to the dummy again. There might be many of these reversals during this step, but patience and repetition will overcome them.

Should the dog persist in refusing to pick up the dummy when the hand is not touching it, there are two ways to coax the dog along. One way is to make a sling for the dummy by tying the two ends of a piece of string to the dummy, one to each end. Another string can be tied to the sling and the dummy can be lowered in front of the dog to head height. The arrangement is similar to that described for lowering a bird in a net in step 13 in training for "whoa". The dummy can gradually be lowered to the table or floor.

Another method that can be used is to set two bricks on end so the dummy can rest on the top of the bricks. Then set the bricks on edge with the dummy resting across them. Then lay the bricks flat. Then set the dummy on the table top with the bricks flanking the dummy. Finally the bricks can be removed completely. In both techniques the pointing finger will probably be required on the first lessons.

Picture 37. First step in teaching the dog to pick up the dummy without the trainer holding it. Lay the dummy on the table with just the fingers of the right hand touching it. Then, after several successful pick ups, just the forefinger touching the dummy. Pudelpointer. (Photo by Edward Bailey).

Picture 38. First step in teaching the dog to take a step (to move off the "whoa") to pick up the dummy. Place the dummy on the table so he must stretch to reach it without moving his feet. Then the dummy is placed at a greater distance so he must take a step to reach it. Again the pointing finger and pinching of the ear in some cases might be required. Pudelpointer. (Photo by Edward Bailey).

Step 6.

Only when the dog is picking up the dummy quickly on the command to "fetch" with a minimum of visual clues from the trainer's hand should the dog be made to move to pick up the dummy. The dog has been whoaed and only the command "come" can make him move. However, later when hunting, the handler will want the dog to whoa when the bird is flushed and to leave whoa and retrieve quickly when the command "fetch" is given. Therefore at this step in his training, the dog must begin to learn that "fetch" is another release from "whoa".

The dummy is placed on the table top in front of the dog so he must stretch to reach it without moving his feet. The pointing finger might be needed the first few times. Then the dummy is placed at a greater distance so he must take a step to reach it (picture 38). Again the pointing finger and pinching of the ear might be required in some cases. If the dog is reluctant to move because he has been whoaed so thoroughly, some urging with "come", "fetch" might be required.

The dummy is gradually moved farther away so the dog must take 2 or 3 steps. Each time the dog picks up the dummy he must hold it until commanded "out". The handler should move with the dog so as to be right beside him to receive the dummy (picture 39).

Picture 39. The dummy is gradually moved farther away so the dog must take 2 or 3 steps. The handler should move with the dog so as to be right beside him to receive the dummy. German Shorthaired Pointer. (Photo by Vern Brand).

STEP 7.

This step, the dog carrying the dummy, need not follow Step 6 but can be interspersed with any step from Step 2 onward. When the dog is holding the dummy for extended periods with teasing by tapping, or grasping the dummy, and not releasing it until the "out" is given and all preceding steps are also mastered with the dog on the floor or ground, carrying can begin.

The dog is off the table and holding the dummy. Command "come" and lead the dog at a walk. Expect the dog to drop the dummy on the command "come". Prevent the dog from dropping it by holding it in his mouth while repeating "fetch", "fetch". When the dog has carried the dummy a few yards, command "whoa", make certain the dog holds the dummy and then "out". If the dog should attempt to drop the dummy, prevent him from doing so and command "fetch" again. When he holds it for a few moments, command "out". Repeat with walking, then trotting, then leading the dog onto the table and down off again. Again, when the dog starts down the ramp he will probably attempt to drop the dummy (pictures 40 and 41). Again, prevent it.

The dummy must be kept in the dog's mouth. Each time the trainer needs to correct the dog to prevent dropping the dummy the command "fetch" should be given. Do not tell the dog "hold it" or any other command except fetch. Fetch means the whole sequence of the retrieve. Additional words only confuse the issue and give the dog added things to learn which are not necessary.

Eventually the trainer should be able to lead the dog at a walk and then trot and lead him up onto the table and down off again and jumping low hurdles without the dog dropping the dummy. If the dog is being difficult, the chin strap on the dummy can be secured. This holds the dummy in the dog's mouth so he can't drop it and makes the task less tiring on the handler's back. The chin strap should not be so tight as to pinch the dog, but just tight enough to keep the dummy held behind the lower canine teeth (picture 42).

STEP 8.

Progressing to heavy dummy can be attempted only when Step 5 is well mastered. The dog should be picking up the light dummy from the table with no hesitation by this time. Begin with the heavy dummy weighing only a pound. Place the dummy on the table, command "fetch". If the dog first hesitates when feeling the unexpected weight, again command "fetch" more firmly and reinforce the command by pointing. Do not put the heavy dummy into the dog's mouth because the dog is expecting the light weight dummy. The sudden surprise of a heavier weight might cause the dog to drop it. And this is something you do not wish to cultivate.

When the dog is picking up and carrying the dummy off the table without dropping it, the weight can very gradually be increased until the dog is carrying 10 to 12 pounds. The increase in weight must not exceed the dog's physical

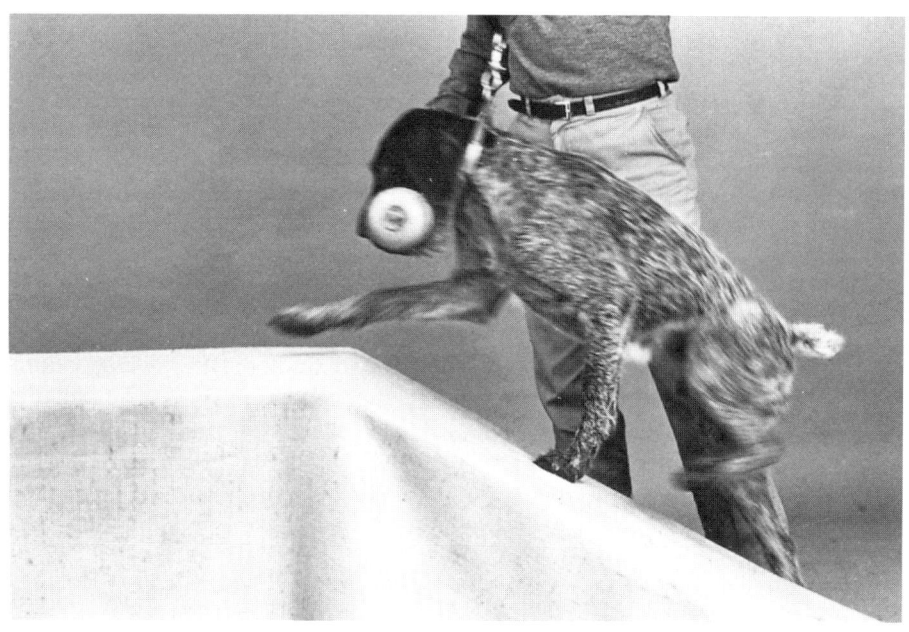

Pictures 40 (above) and 41 (below). Early stages of teaching the dog to carry the retrieve object. After the dog has learned to carry the dummy on the ground while walking and trotting, lead him onto the table and down off, being sure to prevent him from dropping the dummy, especially when he starts down the ramp. German Wirehaired Pointer. (Photos by Vern Brand).

development, however. The trainer must use his own judgement of the dog's capability. A dog should not be carrying the heaviest weights before he has attained full growth, development of neck muscles and is physically capable.

Most dogs enjoy carrying the heavier dummy and assume a proud, "show-off" posture. Usually, they are much more apt to perform flawlessly with the heavier weight. However, when hunting later on, they will be expected to retrieve light and heavy game with equal facility, so they must be taught now that they must do both equally.

STEP 9.

Repeat Step 5 off the table on the ground or floor. If the dog refuses to pick up the dummy, repeat preceding Steps 1 through 4 until the dog understands he must perform off the table as he did on it. Usually there is not so much difficulty at this time because the dog is already whoaing, coming and carrying the dummy while off the table so the transition from picking up the dummy from the table top to picking it up from the ground or floor is not too great.

Have the dog carry the dummy as in Step 7 using dummies of various weights as in Step 8. Repeat Step 6 requiring the dog to move a few steps to pick up the dummy. The dog should not be dropping the dummy by now, even when walking or trotting. Only when the command "out" is given should the dog relinquish his hold on the dummy.

Picture 42. If the leather chin strap on the dummy has to be used with a difficult dog during the retrieving lessons, be sure the strap is not so tight as to pinch the dog. It should be just tight enough to keep the dummy held behind the lower canine teeth. German Wirehaired Pointer. (Photo by Paul Bouchard).

Step 10.

Until now, the dog has always had the trainer immediately beside him when picking up the dummy. He must now begin going out away from the handler, pick up a dummy and return it to the handler.

The dog already should be accustomed to moving a few steps with the handler beside him holding the leash. Begin by whoaing the dog. *Carry, DO NOT TOSS,* the dummy out 3 or 4 feet in front of the dog and place it on the ground. Return to beside the dog, hold the leash loosely. Command "fetch". Ideally, the dog will go to the dummy and pick it up and turn to face you. Quickly haul the dog back, steering him straight back with the leash (picture 43).

However, if the dog hesitates to go to the dummy the handler should take a quick step toward the dummy at the same time giving the "fetch" command. If the dog again hesitates, the handler might need to walk the dog to the dummy or even employ slight ear pinching (picture 44). If so, the dog should be led directly back to the starting point immediately after he picks up the dummy. Turn the dog around to face where the dummy was placed and command "out". Praise the dog and repeat the lesson, again attempting to urge him to fetch the dummy while the handler remains motionless.

Keep repeating this step until the dog is going out the full length of the short leash and returning promptly and directly with minimum guidance by the leash. Now change to the long leash, gradually increasing the distance by increments of a few feet until the dog is going out the full length of the long leash, to 30 feet, and returning promptly and directly. Again, carry out the dummy, do not throw it. No wandering or hesitation on the return should be allowed, the more prompt and direct the return the better.

The method of delivery is taught during this step also. The exact style of the delivery is mostly personal preference. One way is to have the dog return, pass the handler on the right side, turn behind the handler and sit or stand by the handler's left leg, holding the retrieved object until told "out". The advantage to this method is the dog is already aligned to the front for a second retrieve or to go out to search. The advantage to having the dog sit before giving up the dummy is only one of control before the next command is given. The advantage of having the dog remain standing is the dog doesn't have to sit down in snow or mud or water unnecessarily.

Another way of delivery that is equally preferable in the field is simply having the dog approach right up to the front of the handler and either sit or stand holding the retrieved object. Other handlers might prefer to have the dog stand on its hind legs with front feet on the handler's chest to deliver the retrieved object without the handler bending over to take it.

Picture 43. In the early stages of the dog learning to go out away from the handler to pick up the dummy, the dog is on the leash. The handler whoas the dog, then carries the dummy out 3 or 4 feet, places it on the ground, and returns to the dog. Command "fetch" as soon as the dog picks up the dummy and turns to face the handler, quickly haul the dog back, steering him straight back with the leash. Pudelpointer. (Photo by Joan Bailey).

Picture 44. If the dog hesitates a great deal on the command to "fetch", the handler might need to walk the dog to the dummy. After the dog picks up the dummy, return him immediately to the starting place and command "out". Pudelpointer. (Photo by Joan Bailey).

Whichever delivery is chosen is a matter of personal preference, but it should be taught from the beginning in this step. Bringing the dog around the back to the side or straight to the front is accomplished by steering with the short leash. Continuous repetition of the delivery, always the same way, will establish the pattern the dog will use. However, each repetition must be the same. Allowing first one way, then another brings on confusion and sloppy work. Be consistent.

An important thing to remember is that "whoa", "come", "fetch", and "out" are all proceeding together. Lessons should be varied, switching from one to the other.

STEP 11.

The dog should now be performing well on the long and short leashes and with both light and heavy dummies. The dummies should be continuously varied. Wrapping the dummies with fur and/or bird wings will get the dog used to picking up furred and feathered game later on. Other objects should be used in place of the dummies such as empty bottles, pieces of wood and finally frozen and unfrozen carcasses of birds and mammals. Personal items such as car keys or gloves should also be used. The dog must learn that when sent to retrieve something, he must return with that object, whatever it is, but he must retrieve it.

STEP 12.

When the dog is performing flawlessly on the leash he can be sent to retrieve when off the leash. The process should be the same as when on leash, starting first with a relatively short retrieve of 4 to 5 yards. Be sure this is attempted first where there is a minimum of distraction and where the dog cannot get away. It would be foolish to attempt the first free retrieve in an open field. A fenced yard or in the basement is best for a start.

As in Step 10, whoa the dog, carry out and place the dummy; return to the dog and then send him by commanding "fetch". If the dog has learned his lessons well he will perform well. In the event the dog does not perform the retrieve satisfactorily, return to using the leash for a few more times.

The "coming in" method is often helpful in encouraging the dog that is reluctant to go out for the retrieve object when off the leash. Whoa the dog and back away from him. Place the dummy 3 or 4 feet in front of the dog and continue backing away in the same direction so you continuously face the dog. When about 10 feet beyond the dummy, stop, command "fetch". The dog is then fetching while coming in toward the trainer and seeing the trainer all the time. The distances can be increased gradually and the dog's confidence is gradually increased.

Increase the distance gradually as done previously while the dog was on the leash until the retrieves are as long as your available space will allow and as long as the dog can see where the dummy was placed.

STEP 13.

The dog must now learn to search in the general direction of where the retrieve object was last seen. Obviously, when hunting, the dog will rarely be able to see downed game from any distance, so he must learn to search for it. For this he uses both nose and eyes.

Whoa the dog, carry the dummy out of sight of the dog, around a corner of a building, behind shrubs, or into another room. Immediately out of sight, drop the dummy and return to the dog using a circuitous route if possible. When back beside the dog command "fetch" and point in the direction of where the dummy was placed. Be sure the dog is facing in the direction he should go before sending him. Make the first attempts short and uncomplicated. The dog should be successful on his first attempt. If not successful, return the dog to the original place, hold him on "whoa" and move the dummy to where it is just visible to the dog and repeat the fetch sequence as in previous steps.

It will only be a short while before the dog begins following the trainer's tracks to the dummy. When he does successfully follow the track to the dummy, the dummy can be dropped while walking with the dog so the dog doesn't see it dropped. Continue on for 10 to 20 yards, stop and send the dog to fetch from the back track. Exercises such as this will add variety to the lessons and make them less boring for the dog, and he will be learning retrieving all the time. However, retrieving is never a game; it must always remain on an absolute basis. The handler must never treat it as play or allow play in retrieving.

At this time the dog can begin getting used to marking falling retrieve objects combined with searching for the object. Now a dummy may be thrown. First throw the dummy so it falls in view of the dog, then toss it so it falls into high grass or weeds or behind a bush. An assistant can toss a dummy from the side and the dog can be introduced to shooting with a dummy falling. The shot should be a cap pistol or blank starting pistol. The bang sound is more to get the dog's attention than to accustom him to loud shooting. Insist that the dog go to retrieve only when ordered and do not tolerate any sloppiness on the retrieve. Remember, retrieving is all serious business and never an occasion for playing.

STEP 14.

The versatile hunting dog must also retrieve game that might be crippled by tracking it, overtaking it, catching and returning it. To accomplish this with assurity, the dog must learn to concentrate on the track and use the track to find the game.

To cultivate this type of blind retrieve, a dead and cold bird or mammal is dragged through grass, woods, and even over some bare ground. If a bird is used, a few feathers are pulled to mark the starting place. A string is attached to the bird's neck and the bird is dragged for 30 to 50 yards over a

Picture 45. The dog is shown the feathers at the start of the drag track and commanded "fetch". German Wirehaired Pointer. (Photo by Edgar Spencer).

Picture 46. (below) The handler lets the dog lead him on the track. German Wirehaired Pointer. (Photo by Henry Tanzer).

Pictures 47 (above) and 48 (below). The handler continues to let the dog lead him on the track. He must keep the dog calm and on the track urging "fetch" each time the dog shows intensity and concentration on the track and praise often. German Wirehaired Pointer. (Photos by Edgar Spencer).

premarked course or along a mowed path. A shorter drag track should be used if the dog is difficult. Dragging through heavy dew or frost is equally good. The drag trail must be visible to the handler as he must steer the dog, keeping him on the trail. The bird is left at the end of the drag trail and the dragger continues to walk for another 10-20 yards, then returns by a circuitous route on the down wind side of the track. The dog should remain close to the starting point so he is able to see the laying of the drag track. The handler brings the dog up on the long leash, but attached to the collar so it is not choking the dog.

The dog is shown the feathers and commanded "fetch" (picture 45). The handler then lets the dog lead him on the track (pictures 46, 47, 48). The handler must keep the dog calm and on the track urging "fetch" each time the dog shows intensity and concentration on the track and praise often. On reaching the bird the dog is again told "fetch" and as soon as he picks up the bird, the handler should run with the dog giving lots of praise back to the starting point before commanding "out".

The next time a track is to be run, the track should be made as before. The long leash should not be snapped to the collar but instead be slipped under it leaving two ends in the trainers hand (picture 49). The dog should be commanded "fetch" as before and should lead the handler down the track. When the dog shows concentration and is moving along the track, the handler stops and releases one end of the leash while holding the other end (picture

Picture 49. The long leash is slipped under the collar, leaving two ends in the trainer's hand. German Wirehaired Pointer. (Photo by Henry Tanzer).

50). The dog should continue on, the leash slipping unnoticed from under the collar (picture 51).

The calm tracking dog should continue on to the bird and retrieve it. A more excited dog less inclined toward tracking might leave the track and start searching. If so, command the dog to whoa and call him back to the track with "come", replace the leash and attempt it again. Such dogs should be worked for a longer period of time on the long leash over the same marked drag path, but not more than twice a day, then twice a week when he begins to perform well, until the dog stays with the drag track. Continue making tracks of various lengths until the dog can be shown the starting point and with one command to fetch, will move down the track to the bird and retrieve it quickly.

The dog may carry his nose low to the track or high on the downwind side of the track. This does not matter. What is important is that the dog use the track to find the retrieve object. Equally, it doesn't matter whether the dog uses the scent of the dragged bird or the scent of the dragger's tracks. Concentration on the track is what must be learned no matter what the track is.

The length and directions of the track should be increased and changed so the dog eventually is following a track with curves in it for several hundred yards and so the dog goes out of sight of the handler and still always returns with the dragged object. If the dog returns without the retrieve object, he should be shown the start point again and shaken roughly by the collar, told sternly to "fetch" and be sent on the track. If he again fails to retrieve when it is possible to retrieve the dragged object, the track should be made short again so the handler can see the end and all steps must be repeated. Failure to retrieve from the track should never be allowed to go uncorrected.

Teaching a dog to follow a drag will not in any way interfere with his normal field work. It will not turn a highheaded dog into a lowheaded one searching for footscent. Remember, never lay a drag into the wind. Avoid sharp turns. Never make U-turn like drags. Always proceed in one direction. Also never return on the drag track or on upwind side. After depositing the drag object continue for about 10-20 yards in the same direction, then return by a circuitous route.

STEP 15.

Retrieving of dead game not shot over the dog is a valuable attribute to cultivate in the versatile dog. The well trained dog will pick up and retrieve any animal he finds dead with little or no schooling. However, this can be encouraged quite easily. Carry a few dead and cold birds such as pigeons in a pocket or sack when taking the dog through a field or woods. When the dog is out ahead and not looking at you, toss a bird out, mark its approximate location and continue on. Toss out 2 or 3 more in the same manner. After about a half hour, return with the dog, keeping to the down wind side of each bird so the dog can pick up the scent.

Picture 50. When the dog shows concentration and is moving along the track, the handler stops and releases one end of the leash while holding the other end. German Wirehaired Pointer. (Photo by Edgar Spencer).

Picture 51. The dog should continue on, the leash slipping unnoticed from under the collar. German Wirehaired Pointer. (Photo by Henry Tanzer).

As each bird is approached, the dog should scent it and go to it. If the dog does not pick it up and retrieve it, but does indicate he has located it, command "fetch". If the dog has been well prepared through all steps of retrieving, he will retrieve it immediately. Continue until all birds are recovered. Praise the dog well each time he locates and retrieves. Do not give the command to fetch unless it is necessary. The dog is learning to pick up and bring every dead bird or animal he finds and he should do so without command. Only give the command if he hesitates to pick up and retrieve the birds. In this case as in all phases of training, unnecessary commands should be left unspoken.

The dog that retrieves dead with no command is a cooperative dog. He is doing a job for his master and should always receive lavish praise for it. Even if the dead game he brings is pretty high, do not show any displeasure. Praise him lavishly each time he delivers anything, no matter what it is or how bad it might smell. He is trying to please you and you must show your pleasure.

The retrieve of shot game is an absolute essential in any versatile hunting dog. A dog that does not perform equally well both before and after the shot is not living up to his potential as a versatile hunting dog. Retrieving is serious business and must always be treated as such — never as play. For this reason, force training for the retrieve is the only route to follow.

As with training for whoa and come, no set number of lessons or set time can be specified. The speed of progress must be dictated by the individual dog. Proceed one step at a time and go to step 2 only after step 1 is mastered.

Though a step by step procedure might appear slow, each step builds on the preceding step. Do not skip any steps; there are no short cuts. Do not get out of sequence or unnecessary difficulties will arise. In the long run, the trainer will get his reward with every retrieve the dog makes, the easy ones as well as the difficult.

SUMMARY OF THE FETCH SEQUENCE:

1. Holding the dummy for short periods on the table.
2. Reaching for the dummy.
3. Picking up and carrying the dummy.
4. Progressing to heavier dummies.
5. Picking up and carrying the heavy dummy.
6. Going out from the trainer to pick up the dummy and returning on the leash.
7. Going out from the trainer and retrieving the dummy off the leash.
8. Retrieving unseen dummy — blind retrieve.
9. Extended blind retrieve from a drag track.

Chapter 4

RETRIEVING FROM WATER

The versatile hunting dog should retrieve from land or water with equal facility. He should be equally useful in searching a field or woods with a strong desire, pointing and retrieving shot game and yet should be sitting quietly beside or in a blind when desired or sneaking quietly by the hunter's side when stalking to a pond for jump shooting waterfowl. He should enter water unhesitatingly to make a retrieve or swim across a water course to retrieve from the far side.

EQUIPMENT REQUIRED:
1. Short leash 6 feet flat leather.
2. Long leash 30 feet flat webbing.
3. Chain choke collar.
4. Light weight floating dummy.
5. Proper water conditions.
6. Variety of dead birds.

STEP 1.

Before the dog can be expected to retrieve from water, he must have no fear of the water. Proper introduction of the dog to water should take place long before retrieving lessons at the water are begun. Some dogs never have any fear of water, some develop a fear of it and some fear it from the very beginning. The versatile hunting dog with good potential will immediately enter water with no hesitation the first time he is exposed to it. However, accidents or handler blunders at this early time can cause the dog to fear it and might, in fact, ruin the dog for good water work.

A puppy can be introduced to water from 10 weeks of age onward. If the weather is warm, the puppy can first be led — not on the leash, but running freely with the handler — through warm puddles. Allow the pup to play around the water getting his feet wet, the more he splashes about the better. If possible, on a later outing with the pup, locate a small, shallow, but moving stream, large enough so the pup must wade through it but small enough for the handler to step across it easily (picture 52). When the handler crosses, the pup should follow with no hesitation. If the pup hesitates, the handler should keep on going, forcing the pup to follow or be left. If the pup absolutely refuses to wade across, the handler must not force the dog and never push the dog into the water, carry it in or in anyway physically force the dog. Coaxing or urging by the handler is seldom of any help at this point.

If the dog shows this fear of water early in its life and not having had any bad experiences with water, it indicates timidness in the dog. A timid dog is more difficult to train in every respect and will never be a strong hunter with high desire to work. Extreme cases can become little more than heartbreak or at best, wasted time for the trainer.

Picture 52. Trainer takes older dog and young pup for walk, crossing shallow stream so that the pup must follow. The water is shallow enough so that the pup does not have to swim. Griffon. (Photo by Edward Bailey).

If the dog shows no fear of water in which it can wade, take it to a shallow pond with a gradual descent into swimming depth water. A steep bank with sudden drop off could intimidate the dog. The handler can wade into the water, gradually leading the dog into deeper water until he swims.

An easier way is to have another dog (the pup's mother and littermates are good if possible) that goes into water with no hesitation. Usually a pup will follow. Best and easiest with a somewhat fearful dog that has reached 3 or 4 months of age is a live, wing-clipped duck released onto the water with 2 or 3 other dogs available as chasers. Providing the water is deep enough for the duck to dive and too large for the reticent pup to keep running around it, allow all the dogs to chase the duck. The pup will almost certainly get so excited he will forget his fear of water and join the chase (pictures 53 and 54).

Another way to get a dog over fear of water is for the handler to go swimming himself, taking the dog with him. If the water is warm enough for the handler, it should present no problem for the dog. The handler should first wade along the edge, letting the pup walk with him, gradually the handler can wade into deeper water while encouraging the dog until both dog and handler are swimming.

There are many other ways to overcome fear of water, but if the young dog is introduced properly, he should have a real love for it and never develop fear.

Picture 53. This flowing stream allows enough room for the wing-clipped duck to out maneuver the older and younger dog. This young dog had been fearful of the water, but with the released duck and the excitement of the older dog, the young dog took to the water quickly. Griffon. (Photo by Edward Bailey).

Picture 54 (below). Here a large pond is put to the same use, as the young dog pursues the duck. (Photo by Edward Bailey).

57

Step 2.

Assuming the dog has no fear of water and swims willingly, and if the dog has proceeded through all the steps of retrieving on land, retrieving from water can begin. The dog should know thoroughly the commands "fetch", "out", "whoa" and "come" and should be retrieving unerringly on land before going to the water.

Lead the dog to the edge of a pond with a gradually sloping bottom. Whoa the dog at a clear place by the water's edge where no brush or high weeds hinder the dog's visibility. Carry the dummy out into the water 5 or 6 feet to where water depth will not require the dog to swim. Lay the dummy on the water and return to the dog's side. The dog should be on the long leash in this step.

When beside the dog, command "fetch" and take a step forward while pointing toward the dummy (picture 55). The dog should respond just as he has on land because he is not yet swimming. However, picking up a floating dummy might cause a problem. If the dog hesitates to pick it up, command "fetch" more sternly. The lessons on retrieving on land, if adequately done, should have the dog thoroughly prepared and no problem should arise and in most cases will not arise. If the dog should refuse, go to the dog, support the dummy with the hand while commanding "fetch". The dog will most likely grasp it then. Require the dog to carry the dummy to dry land by leading the dog back on the long leash (picture 56). Do not allow the dog to drop the dummy before the command "out" is given.

On the next repetition of the lesson, place the dummy at the water's edge so it is just in the water resting on the bottom. The dummy, having a more firm surface under it will be less confusing and give the dog no trouble. Progress very gradually to deeper water.

If the dog has gone to the dummy and picked it up with no difficulty, the handler should move back 2 or 3 yards from the water's edge as the dog is returning with the dummy. If the dog indicates he wants to put down the dummy at the edge of the water, command "fetch" and run quickly away from the water leading the dog on the leash. Do not use unnecessary commands such as "no" or "hold it". "Fetch" alone means the whole sequence. The handler may expect and should have delivery of the dummy just as in previous lessons in retrieving on land.

If the dog should not want to return immediately with the dummy, the collar and long leash are used just as was done on the initial phases of retrieving training on land. However, care must be taken to use the leash only in shallow water and be sure the dog does not get tangled in the leash. Becoming tangled could instill an unreasonable fear of water retrieving in the young dog during these early stages of water work.

Picture 55. The first retrieve from water the dog is on the long leash. The dummy is out in shallow water about 5 or 6 feet from shore. Pudelpointer. (Photo by Christa Winterhelt).

Picture 56. Require the dog to carry the dummy to dry land by leading the dog back on the long leash. Do not allow the dog to drop the dummy before the command "out" is given. Pudelpointer. (Photo by Christa Winterhelt).

STEP 3.

When the dog has completed successfully the retrieve of the carried out dummy, the handler can now toss the dummy. The distance of the toss should not be much greater than the carried distance and the water depth should still be wading depth but so the dog nearly needs to swim. The retrieve should be as previously in that the dog should return to the handler without stopping to shake and without dropping the dummy. Use of the long leash and collar in this and in the preceding step is essential to keep the dog from learning that the handler has less control when the dog is in water. The use of the leash also prevents the dog from stopping to shake or to drop the dummy when coming from water onto the land.

The handler can now move the dog back from the water's edge 2 or 3 yards so part of the distance to the dummy is on land and part over water. Continue to demand correct performance on every retrieve. Mistakes are to be corrected immediately.

With dog and handler back 2 to 3 yards from the water's edge, the dummy can now be tossed into swimming depth water. Continue to use the long leash as far as distance allows. If the trainer has brought his dog through steps 2 and 3 correctly, there will be no problem. Gradually increase distance the dog must swim and vary the distance between dog and water's edge. The purpose of this is to introduce variability into the lessons. Vary also the duration of holding the dog, up to 2 or 3 minutes, before commanding "fetch". The dog must not be allowed to break the "whoa" without being commanded to do so. When the distance has been increased to where the long leash can no longer be used, remove the leash and collar. Other than during these early steps of retrieving from water, the collar should always be removed before the dog is sent into water. The danger of getting the collar tangled in some obstacle is too great a risk. As long as the leash is used, the collar presents little danger because the dog can quickly be hauled back in the event of an accidental tangle.

When the dog is retrieving from as far as the dummy can be thrown and still be visible to the dog, the trainer can move away from the whoaed dog to throw the dummy.

The trainer can go off to the side, even out of sight of the dog and throw the dummy so it lands in the water where the dog can see it. Return to the dog before commanding "fetch". This exercise reinforces the early "whoa" lessons so the dog remains where told and gets the dog watching for objects falling into the water. Again, the dog must not be allowed to break. If he does, review of whoa lessons is required. An assistant to throw the dummy while the handler remains by the dog to enforce the whoa is a help at this point.

At this time it is good practice for the dog if a gun is fired when the dummy is tossed. Begin with a small gun such as a .22 blank starting pistol and gradually increase the loudness of the gun used. Shooting during this phase of training both within sight of the dog and when out of sight, will teach the dog to remain quiet while shooting is going on. Later, when used for waterfowl hunting, the dog must be quiet and now is the best time to learn it.

STEP 5.

The dog should be well versed in searching for a hidden dummy on land from his earlier retrieving lessons. He can now start searching for a dummy in the water. Again proceed from the easy to the difficult.

Locate a pond that contains clumps of weeds or brush growing in the water. First, toss the dummy so it lands on the side nearest the dog and just into the weeds. The dog should be able to see it splash. If the dog is successful, repeat the lesson but this time tossing the dummy to the edge on either the right or left side of the weeds. Again repeat, tossing the dummy farther into the weeds and finally to the far side and beyond.

Dead birds can be substituted for the dummy during these lessons. Any bird can be used. Pigeons are the easiest and cheapest to obtain. However, the feathers quickly become soaked so each bird can only be used for 2 or 3 retrieves. Best is a duck if available. A live shackled duck with the bill taped shut can also be used.

STEP 6.

A versatile dog should be expected to retrieve birds shot over decoys. He should learn to do this without getting tangled in the anchor lines and without returning with a decoy instead of the duck he was expected to retrieve.

Set several decoys out on the lawn, basement floor or any place where decoys and dummy will be visible to the dog. Whoa the dog a few yards from the decoys. Carry the dummy to the near side of the decoy set. Return to the dog, command "fetch". The dog should go to the dummy and retrieve it with no delay (picture 57). If the dog attempts to go past the dummy to the decoys, stop the dog with "whoa". Go to the dog, point to the dummy and command "fetch" (picture 58). Require the dog to return the dummy back to the starting place.

Repeat the lesson, putting the dummy first on one side of the decoy set, then the other and eventually beyond the set. Each time the dog must be made to pick up the dummy and must be prevented from picking up a decoy. When the dog shows he is clearly discriminating between decoys and dummy, and he should be after only a few lessons, the dummy can be placed within the decoy set.

The distance can then be increased and dead birds substituted for the dummy. The heavy dummy can also be used to advantage during this step.

STEP 7.

The decoy set can now be moved to a pond and set out and anchored. The anchor lines should be as short as possible to minimize the chance of tangling the dog. Repeat the procedure as was done on land.

Picture 57 (above). First retrieve with decoys is done on land. Set the dummy on the near side of the decoy set. Return to the dog and give the command to "fetch". The dog should go to the dummy and retrieve it with no delay. German Wirehaired Pointer. (Photo by Edgar Spencer).

Picture 58 (left). If the dog attempts to go past the dummy to the decoys, stop the dog with "whoa". Go to the dog, point to the dummy and command "fetch" German Wirehaired Pointer. (Photo by Henry Tanzer).

It is helpful at this time to have a command that means "do not do that". Many use a firm "No", but there is the chance of the dog confusing no and whoa. If such confusion arises, the no can be changed to no no or better to "agh" — a short "a" sound like saying the word "at" but leaving off the t sound. If this is desired, it is best taught on land first, in step 6. However, the "whoa" can be used in water just as it was on the land. The dog should have already associated the "whoa" used in Step 6 with decoys on land with not picking up a decoy.

Do not jump to Step 7 before doing Step 6. The dog must learn the difference between decoys and dummy or dead bird thoroughly before going to the water. If Step 6 is mastered, the dog will have no trouble with Step 7. However, the handler has less control over the dog in water and the clever dog will know that and so might attempt disobedient acts there that he would not dare to do on land.

STEP 8.

Make the retrieves required increasingly difficult. Combine the searching in weeds for a dead bird with the presence of decoys. If the retrieving training has been well learned, the dog knows it must return with something. Many dogs will begin a search for a bird hidden in weeds but abandon it and attempt to retrieve a decoy. The handler should be prepared for this and be ready to stop it before the dog learns to do it. Far better to avoid the formation of a bad habit than to try to correct an already formed one.

At this time the dog can be started to retrieve doubles also. However, the versatile dog is not the good marker one might expect in retriever specialists. He was not meant to be. Rather, the versatile dog should go to the general area of the fallen bird and then search, using his nose to locate the bird. The complete response to the handler's commands to put the retriever on the precise spot should not be expected or required of the versatile dog. The one command "fetch" should be the only command necessary. The dog should do the rest himself.

The dog can be taught to go back during this step. Command "back" and throw a stone so it splashes beyond the dog. If the command "back" always precedes the stone splash by a second or two, the dog will quickly associate the word back with going away from the handler and the stone throw will be required only a few times. The arm movement, as though throwing a stone, can be retained as the hand signal for the verbal command to go back. The same technique can be used for go left or go right if desired. If so desired, all versatile dogs can be taught to obey hand signals. The method used for the retriever specialist is the most logical.

SUMMARY OF RETRIEVING FROM WATER:

1. Introduce the dog to water first so he has no fear of water.
2. Retrieve dummy from wading depth water.
3. Retrieve of thrown dummy from shallow water.
4. Retrieve of thrown dummy from swimming depth water.
5. Searching for and retrieving from emergent cover in water.
6. Retrieving from around and among decoys on land.
7. Retrieving from around and among decoys in water.
8. Searching for and retrieving from weeds in water in presence of decoys.

COMMON MISTAKES:

1. The worst mistake is the handler losing his temper when the dog is hesitant at the water. Throwing the dog in or other undue force can be disastrous.
2. Permitting the dog to lay down the object or game when coming out of the water, if not corrected early in training, could allow loss of crippled game later.

Chapter 5

TRACKING

The versatile hunting dog should also be able to follow the trail of a wounded bird or small mammal and follow the blood trail of a wounded big game animal. The dog can be expected to follow out, off the leash, and retrieve from any distance every wounded small game animal. He should also follow the blood trail, leading the hunter to any wounded big game animal.

The major requirement for the dog is the ability to concentrate on the ground track rather than range out attempting to locate air carried scent in a hit or miss fashion. When the track is faint or the blood trail sparse and cold, the good versatile dog will pick his way carefully along the trail, working it out until the wounded game is located. When the track is strong and fresh, he will move rapidly along it with great efficiency, a quick location and retrieve. The training required for tracking is primarily teaching the dog to concentrate and gauge his speed to the existing conditions.

The versatile hunting dog has a natural ability to track. The ability to concentrate on the track differs from breed to breed and individual to individual. Teaching the dog to concentrate, that is teaching the dog to control his temperament and utilize ground scent, does not in any way interfere with his ability to use air current to find body scent or to run with a high nose. We no more change a high nosed dog to a low nosed dog through training than we can change a low nosed dog such as the hounds to a high nosed dog.

EQUIPMENT REQUIRED:
1. Long leash, 30 feet flat webbing.
2. A variety of dead birds up to pheasant and duck size.
3. A variety of dead small game animals up to jackrabbit size.
4. Live wing clipped pheasants and ducks.

STEP 1.

The first and most basic step in tracking has already been described in Step 14 in the retrieving section. The retrieve from a drag track teaches the dog the concentration aspect as well as how to use his nose to best advantage in the tracking situation. This step 14 of Retrieving should be repeated using a variety of sizes and species of birds and using various mammals. Each animal used should be cold and should be as free of blood as possible. All kinds of furred animals can be used from chipmunk or squirrel to woodchuck, rabbits and up to hares. However, dogs that are being used for bird hunting only should be taught with birds only.

The terrain and length of the track should be varied and failure to successfully work out the track and retrieve must not be allowed. However, the trainer should do everything conceivable to cause the dog to make a mistake. The dog should learn what is not satisfactory as well as what is satisfactory to the trainer. If a dog is punished for making a mistake, he will not repeat it. But, if he is not punished either for a mistake he has made or because he has never had a mistake for which to be punished, he cannot know what he should not do. Better to cause the dog to make a blunder during training and correct him than to have him make a mistake unknowingly later when hunting. The dog must know he is making a mistake when he is punished for it or he should not be punished.

If the dog never fails on the retrieve from the drag track, the trainer must make it impossible for him to succeed. To accomplish this, though it might sound diabolical, an assistant should drag the retrieve animal so the drag track ends at the base of a tree. The drag animal should then be lifted into the tree and secured out of reach and out of sight of the dog and the helper should hide from view. The trainer should start his dog on the track with the command "fetch". The dog failing to locate the animal at the end of the track will return to the trainer empty mouthed. The dog should then be taken to the start of the track again. Show the dog the start point and give a few harsh yanks on the collar. Give a stern command "fetch". The helper should meanwhile have taken the drag animal or bird from the tree and placed it at the end of the track and again hidden himself. This time the dog should succeed on locating the drag animal and making the retrieve. He should then be well praised for his successful work.

STEP 2.

The dog must learn also to follow the track of a running crippled bird. Teaching this to a dog, like the drag track, is also a matter of instilling concentration, thereby improving the efficiency of the dog's innate ability. This work can be done at an early age, as soon as the young dog's pointing has been well established. Pull (do not cut) the last 7 primary feathers from one wing of a pheasant. Tie a brightly colored, light weight line of about 20 feet in length around the base of the wings by passing the end of the line under one wing, across the back in front of the wings, then under the other wing and tie it so the knot is on the center of the bird's back with the long free end trailing (picture 59). Remove some soft feathers from the bird to mark the beginning of the track (picture 60) and release the bird at that spot (picture 61). The bird should run in the direction it was facing, toward heavier cover and should then attempt to hide.

This track should be set in an open field situation with short, moderately open cover but with more dense cover like a fence row or hedge 75 to 100 yards away. The wind should be quartering across the track if possible. Carefully watch the path the bird takes so the dog can be steered on it as it was in the drag track.

Bring the dog to the start of the track with the long leash through the collar as described in step 14 of retrieving. Show the starting place to the

Picture 59. After pulling the last 7 primary feathers from one wing of a pheasant, tie a brightly colored, light weight line of about 20 feet around the base of the wings so the knot is on the center of the bird's back with the long free end trailing. (Photo by Edward Bailey).

Picture 60. Remove some soft feathers from the bird to mark the beginning of the track. (Photo by Vern Brand).

Picture 61. Release the bird at the spot where you pulled out the soft feathers. The bird should run in the direction it was facing, toward heavier cover and should then attempt to hide. (Photo by Vern Brand).

dog and command "fetch". Calm the dog and keep working him onto the track. Keep working the dog on the leash the whole length of the track until he is intently concentrating on it and showing no tendency toward wandering or otherwise indicating his mind is not on it. Never should the handler run or allow the dog to wildly pull him. Quiet concentration is essential.

When the dog is concentrating on the track and moving purposefully along it (picture 62), the trainer can stop and let the leash slip from under the collar allowing the dog to proceed along the track. If the dog turns from the track and starts searching, call him in and again put him on the long leash to steer him on the track.

If the dog should point the bird when coming to it, he should not be faulted. Go up to the dog, praise him and pick up the bird. If the dog moves in and catches the bird and retrieves it, praise him. Do not reprimand him for moving in. Catching a bird after tracking it will not harm his point. Later, under hunting conditions the dog will be expected to track down and retrieve a wing-tipped bird, he will be expected to catch it when it is running. The tracking training is meant to prepare him for this task.

Picture 62. Once the dog is concentrating on the track of the live pheasant, and he is moving purposefully along it, the trainer can stop and let the leash slip from under the collar allowing the dog to proceed along the track. German Wirehaired Pointer. (Photo by Edgar Spencer).

STEP 3.

A truly versatile dog is expected to also follow the scent trail left by a duck swimming through both open water and water with a lot of emergent vegetation. Preparation of the dog for this task is similar to the tracking on land and follows a similar sequence. The facilities required are more extensive, however.

Locate a small pond or slough with some emergent vegetation around it. A live duck is required. Domesticated mallards can be purchased for this purpose. Pull the primary feathers from one wing so the duck is rendered flightless. Place the duck on the ground 5 to 10 yards from the edge of the water, remove some soft feathers to mark the release spot and let the duck walk toward the pond. When the duck has entered the water and has gotten hidden from view, bring up the dog. Show him the starting spot and command "fetch". The collar should be removed for this as in all water working. The practice on the drag track and the live bird track will have prepared the dog for following the land trail of the duck. The dog should enter the water and keep following the water trail until he catches the duck or chases it into deep open water. If the dog cannot catch the duck, the duck can be shot and the dog ordered to retrieve. Obviously, care should be taken to shoot only when the dog is far from the duck.

STEP 4.

Blood tracking is the specialization of the hound. But most versatile breeds had hound in their ancestry at some time, and so it is not too much to expect that they should be able to follow a blood trail. Training for following a blood trail can begin after the dog's retrieving training has been completed. Blood can usually be obtained from a slaughter house and cattle blood can serve as well as any. Collect about a quart of fresh blood, shake it well, let it clot, then filter it through cloth or a fine meshed screen to remove the clots, into a clean plastic squeeze bottle or any bottle which can deliver the blood a drop or two at a time. Sprinkle 10 to 15 drops at the starting place, then 1 or 2 drops at each 1 yard interval in a relatively straight line for 100 yards. The course should be well marked so the trainer knows exactly where the trail is located. At about the 100 yard mark again sprinkle 10 to 15 drops and make a bend in the track of about 30 degrees. Continue for another hundred yards with one drop at each 1 yard interval. Again, the trail should be well marked for the trainer. Sprinkle 10 to 15 drops at the 200 yard point, make a bend and continue as before.

For the first attempt, a 200 or 300 yard trail is quite sufficient. It can be lengthened on subsequent sessions. Some relatively large animal such as a dead jack rabbit, or similar sized animal is placed at the end of the trail. The blood trail should go through various habitat such as an open brush area and through open or dense woods, as well as open fields and even over bare ground.

Wait 4 or 5 hours and bring the dog with the long leash snapped to a broad leather collar or a chain collar but not choking collar. Start with the dog held short, 3 or 4 feet, show the dog the start and direct him with the leash so he is picking his way carefully from one blood spot to the next. Keep calming the dog continuously so all his attention is directed toward the blood trail. Gradually allow more leash between trainer and dog until the dog is moving on the trail 20 to 25 feet ahead of the trainer. Insist that the dog follow only the series of blood drops and is paying attention to nothing else. Make the dog stop with a "whoa", walk to him, praise him, then encourage him to continue.

Allow the dog to lead the trainer down the trail, being sure the dog makes each turn correctly with minimal overrunning. Keep praising the dog and calming him the whole way. Praise him well when he leads you to the game laid at the end of the track.

Chapter 6

SITTING AND STAYING QUIETLY AT A PRECISE SPOT FOR EXTENDED PERIODS

Many times in the course of normal hunting, the versatile dog must remain quietly sitting or lying at some precise place while the handler is out of sight. This situation arises in waterfowl hunting particularly when the dog is placed outside a blind while the handler is hidden. Or, more difficult for the dog, is being placed on one side of a pond with the handler on another side. The dog must stay quietly waiting no matter how many ducks fly over or fall to the gun until told he can make the retrieve. Many other occasions will call for this particular disciplined behavior, and the dog should be prepared for it.

EQUIPMENT REQUIRED:
1. Chain choke collar
2. Short leash
3. Long leash
4. Object to leave laying by the dog such as a jacket, hat, a leash etc.

STEP 1.

After the dog is finished on "whoa" and is well along in his retrieving exercises, the dog should be introduced to the command "sit". This command should not be taught before "whoa" or before the dog is doing well on tracking exercises. If the dog learns that a tug upward and backward means "sit", teaching "whoa" and teaching concentration on a track are made extremely difficult because the dog sits everytime the leash is tugged. The dog becomes confused and the handler becomes frustrated and must start from the very beginning again.

Sit can be taught best and easiest when the dog is holding the retrieving dummy in his mouth after returning from the pick-up. The dog is standing whoaed beside the handler — on the handler's left side if he is right handed, on the right side if he is left handed — and holding the dummy in his mouth. Press down on the dog's rump using the tips of the fingers, not the flat palm of the hand and with the other hand pull up on the collar with slight but steady pressure. Do not use the choke, use the whole collar. The purpose of pulling up on the collar is just to keep the dog's head up so he doesn't lie down. At the moment the dog's rump is pressed, command "sit". Again, the dog can hear quite well so there is no need to yell.

If this sit lesson is combined with holding the dummy, the handler must also make sure the dummy is not dropped. Praise the dog for sitting and holding, then command "out" and take the dummy and again praise the dog. Both "come" and "fetch" can be used as release commands from "sit." But, never make the dog come from the sit position unless the handler is right beside the dog. Never call the sitting dog if he is out of sight of the handler.

The first lessons in sit can be given on the table or on the floor or ground. If started on the table, it must also be followed by repetitions on the floor and outside on the ground.

STEP 2.

After the dog sits on command, without being pushed on the rump, the handler commands "sit" and lays some object beside the dog, an object like a jacket, a towel or an extra leash etc. The dog is sitting with the short leash attached to the collar. The handler then backs away toward the front of the dog repeating the command "sit-stay". Move to the extent of the leash, then toward one side of the dog, then around front to the other side. Keep repeating "sit-stay" quietly, but firmly. Return to the dog and praise him and pick up the object that was left and tell the dog to "come". Move to another location and repeat the command "sit". Again place the object beside the dog and back off the length of the leash. Move completely around the dog repeating "sit-stay". If the dog attempts to get up to follow, quickly go to the dog and replace him in the exact spot with a firm "sit-stay" command.

When the dog is remaining quietly sitting while the handler moves all around the dog, change to the long leash and repeat the lesson getting gradually farther from the dog. Next let the leash drop out to the front of the dog and continue to walk around the dog. Then attempt the lesson with the dog off the leash.

STEP 3.

The handler should now be able to go out of sight of the dog. Sit the dog by the corner of the house or some small building, leave the object beside the dog with the command "sit-stay". The handler then walks around the house so he can get to watch the dog from behind without the dog seeing him. Care should be taken so the wind is not blowing the scent of the handler to the dog. The handler remains quiet for an extended period until the dog makes an attempt to get up to follow.

The instant the dog attempts to move, the handler must quickly get to the dog and correct him sharply. This tactic can only be repeated the same way once or twice before the dog realizes the handler has gone around and is watching from behind. Therefore, the direction and location must be changed frequently.

Require the dog to sit quietly beside the object left beside him for several minutes, then return to the dog by retracing the course back around the building. Pick up the object left there and praise the dog lavishly before taking the dog from the spot. Never take the dog from the spot without first picking up the object. The dog must make the association between the object left beside him and staying with it. The object anchors him to the spot and he must not leave the place until the object is picked up.

In this exercise, if the dog is repeatedly disobedient, he should be corrected. The handler should always remain calm while correcting behavior.

The leash is left on the dog, he is ordered "sit-stay" and the handler disappears again. The dog's wait should be short, 2 or 3 minutes only, and the handler should return to the waiting dog. Praise the dog lavishly at this time, pick up the object and move the dog on to another aspect of training or end the lessons for the time being.

The dog will learn quickly that to leave the object left beside him means punishment and is not worth trying. He will also learn that the handler will always return for him. The handler can now introduce distractions such as making noises, banging things, slamming doors etc. and the handler can shoot off a light gun or blank pistol. The distractions, especially shooting the gun should be done first in sight of the dog, then out of sight. This "sit-stay" should be repeated at different locations and for varying durations at least once a week after the dog has demonstrated he will sit and stay with distractions.

Common Mistakes:

1. One of the most common mistakes is to attempt this training before the dog is trained on whoaing and retrieving.
2. The worst mistake is to call the dog off the sit-stay without first returning to the dog and picking up the object left there. If the dog is called when out of sight of the handler, the dog becomes uncertain whether the handler will return for him. This causes the dog to creep from the spot or break completely in an attempt to get to the handler.
3. Punishment for mistakes must be dealt out with good timing and forcibly. Soft taps or verbal reprimands accomplish little. When punishment for disobedience is required, it is far kinder to both dog and handler to punish once correctly than to peck away at it indefinitely. Do not make the mistake of hitting a dog with a painless noise maker such as rolled up newspaper.

Chapter 7
SEARCHING FOR GAME

The versatile hunting dog should search in a manner that gives the impression no game has been bypassed, the field has been swept clean. The pace and pattern displayed by the searching dog should not exhaust him but rather can be maintained for a full day of hunting. The versatile hunting dog should not make long unproductive casts, yet should not search the same ground repeatedly or stay so close to the hunter that he must be led into every likely cover by the hunter himself. The dog should show independence in his search but not require hacking or constant correction to keep him in contact. No specific distance between dog and handler can or should be specified. The distance a dog ranges should be dependent on cover, terrain, game being hunted, personal preference and many other things. What applies to the open quail plantation is useless on the woodcock run or the shelterbelt pheasant hunt. The situation dictates distance, not some hard and fast rule.

Similarly, the speed with which a dog covers ground in his search is nonspecific, but will vary with breed and even with individual dogs. The important thing is the dog locates the game, the handler can get to the dog before the game leaves and can flush it and shoot it for the dog to retrieve.

EQUIPMENT REQUIRED:
1. Long leash 30 feet flat webbing.
2. Chain choke collar or leather collar.
3. Open field area.
4. Birds for planting or release.

STEP 1.

Before a young dog is taught a search pattern and use of the wind currents, he must be interested enough in game to want to find it. He must want to search for it. He must also be advanced in his "whoa" lessons so that he can be stopped at any distance. Dogs that are too dependent on the handler cannot be taught to pattern; they must be independent enough so they are not walking beside or behind the handler. Mostly, young dogs will have been taken for romps in a field and either found game and pointed or chased it or found non-game birds such as larks or other birds and chased them. This chasing is not a fault and the dog should not be reprimanded at these early stages.

Dogs that are still hesitant in searching after having found and chased game can be encouraged to show more independence by being taken out at night for a run. Once the dog learns he will not lose his master in the dark, he will be more confident in daylight. However, most well bred versatile dogs will show all the desire they need and will want to search after they have been exposed to game and allowed to chase it.

If, after the dog has chased game and been taken out for runs in the dark, he still shows no enthusiasm for searching, he is a poor prospect for a hunting dog and the trainer's time would be far better spent on a new dog. However, a dog that has spent all his time looking out through the wire of his kennel and has never been introduced to game, cannot be expected to show a great desire to search for game. The dog must be prepared by romps in the field as a puppy and by exposure to the field and to game.

STEP 2.

The dog has been prepared and shows a strong desire to search. The dog must also be well versed in "whoa" and "come". Take the dog to a field where there is no game. The field should have medium cover, not so high as to interfere with visual contact between handler and dog, and not so low as to allow the dog to see small birds or animals in the open. Cover about chest high on the dog is ideal.

The dog is whoaed at the edge of the field about equal distance from each side of the field. The wind should be coming from the opposite end of the field so the forward search will be into the wind. The dog is sent on with the command "Hi-on" or "Hunt-on" or whatever words the handler chooses to mean go out and hunt. Use the same words always, however. The handler moves at a brisk walk, heading at a slight angle into the wind, either to the left or to the right. If the dog has run straight away into the wind, he should be stopped with "whoa" then told "come" so he is also crossing the wind at a slight angle into it and going in the same direction as the handler.

Say the handler has started by going to the right, the dog should be urged to the right so he passes the handler. When he has gotten as far to the right as desired, the handler should turn and head toward the left. Give the "whoa" and "come" commands and walk briskly toward the left so as to quarter across the wind. A wave of the arm in the direction you want the dog to go helps reinforce the direction desired and can be used later when the dog can be expected to respond to hand signals.

Again, the dog passes the handler, going toward the left for the required distance. The dog is whoaed and turned again to the right when he has gone to the left as far as desired. The handler should have again turned toward the right and be walking briskly in that direction. The process is continued until the entire length of the field is traversed. Both handler and dog will make a zig-zag pattern but each arm of the dog's pattern will be two or three times as long as the handler's swings to the left or right (Diagram 2).

Some dogs have this pattern naturally, others need more training. Teaching a dog to systematically pattern in this way also teaches the dog to use the wind to best advantage and encourages cooperation in the hunting situations.

Care should be taken to ensure that the dog always crosses to the front of the handler, not behind. If the handler sees the dog is going to cross behind, he can quickly step back before the dog can pass behind. This encourages the dog to always hunt toward the front.

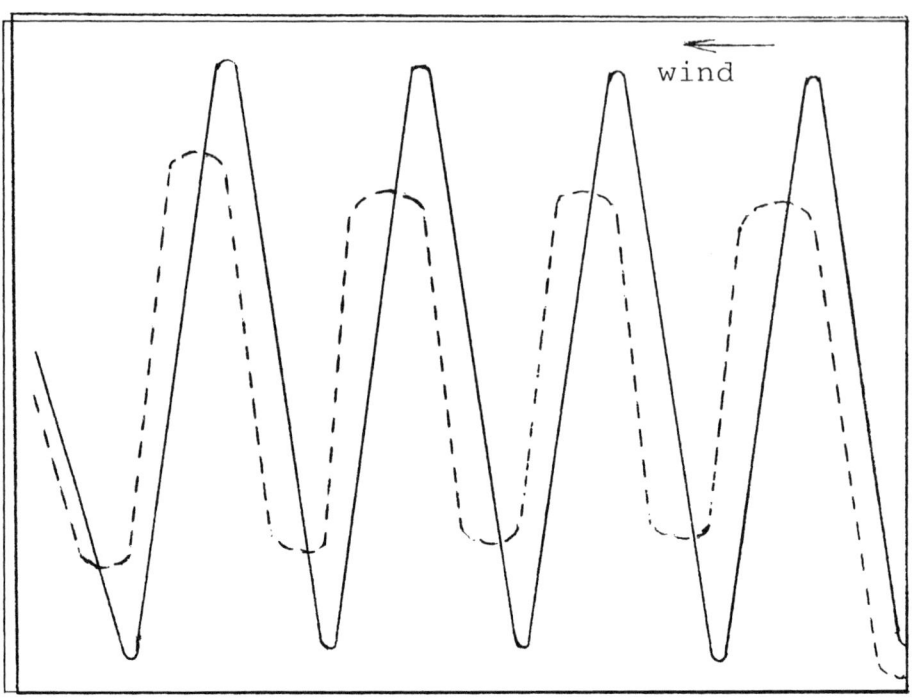

Diagram 2. Establishing the search pattern. The dotted line represents the course of the handler, the solid line is the dog's course. The search starts on the left of the diagram and moves toward the right. The wind direction is from the right toward the left of the diagram.

Should the dog show signs of confusion and discouragement from all the handling and the repeated changes in direction, it is advisable to plant or release a bird for him to get his interest back. But, this should not be done too often because contact with game will only excite the young dog and make the work of both trainer and dog more difficult.

In the early lessons, the work requires concentration by both dog and handler and often requires some brisk movements, even running, on the part of the handler. Also, the finished product cannot be obtained in a few days.

STEP 2.

When the dog has learned to pattern his search so he is reaching out on beyond the handler on each left and right swing, the handler can gradually reduce his own zig-zagging. The dog's desire to work and his developed pattern should keep the dog searching out to the sides as far or as close as the handler wants. Any tendency in the dog to change the pattern indicates he has not yet learned the lessons and more work is needed.

At this time, birds can be planted for the dog, but only if the dog has learned to control his excitement in the presence of game (see Step 13 in

Whoa sequence). To achieve a fluid pattern of covering the ground and not a straight out and back or yo-yo like running which decreases his efficiency, birds should be placed at the far end of the field and toward the sides of the field, not at the start of his search.

Two or three (not more) birds should be planted at several places in the field and about 100 feet apart. When the dog finds the first bird, he can be expected to point it. He should no longer be allowed to chase (see section on steady to flush and shot) when the bird is flushed. Also, he should not be allowed to return to the spot where the bird was after he has moved from the place. Rather, guide the dog, through handling, toward the next bird and then on to the third bird. The dog learns to go find more birds and not return repeatedly to where one was and learns to forget about the one flying away. He soon figures out the fact that there are more birds to be found on the ground.

The handler must employ strict force to prevent the dog from returning to the site of a flush. This is pottering and is wasted time and energy if the dog is allowed to check back on hot spots. Be sure the dog is moved quickly toward a new bird. The same strict force must be applied if the dog attempts to follow the flushed bird. Under no circumstances should the dog be allowed to mark and follow a flushed bird at this stage in training. The handler must control the dog and turn him toward a new bird. Proper application of forcefulness at this point and the dog will readily and willingly accept the order to search for new birds away from the hot spot and away from marked birds in flight. Cooperation in the search is not only requested, it is essential to the effectiveness of dog and handler as a team. The dog must know the handler is the leader of the pack and must be subservient to him, but not mechanically controlled.

COMMON MISTAKES:

1. One common mistake is attempting early training for search in an area where the dog finds a lot of game. A disobedient, overly independent dog will result and set training back to basic obedience lessons.

2. Another common mistake is taking the dog to the field before he is completely trained to whoa and come.

3. Many handlers, fearing their dog will not return when he gets from sight, run after him. This encourages the dog to become more independent and less cooperative.

4. Repeatedly blowing the whistle or yelling whoa when the dog is chasing a flushed bird is a mistake and futile. Wait until the dog returns, put him on the leash and whoa him at the exact place from where the bird flushed.

Chapter 8

POINTING — STEADY TO FLUSH AND SHOT

Pointing is not taught to a dog. The dog is born with the potential for pointing. The trainer can only help develop and direct the potential. The dog is a predatory animal and all predators, including both wild and domesticated members of the dog family — Canidae, pause before springing on prey. In our domestication of the dog, we have taken advantage of this innate pause and selectively bred to lengthen the duration of the pause into what we call pointing. Among all the things we expect of our versatile dogs, pointing staunchly and surely is of major importance. Extreme style is not the important thing to achieve; staunch, solid and above all the productive point is.

EQUIPMENT REQUIRED:

1. Long leash — 30 feet, flat webbing.
2. Old fishing rod with 6 to 8 feet of string or cloth fishing line tied to the end of it.
3. Live quail, pigeon or similar sized bird.

STEP 1.

The dog has already completely learned "whoa", including the final step of being whoaed on the table with the bird in a net in front of him. The dog, having gone through the whoa sequence correctly, is already well on his way to steadiness. But, the emphasis is on correctly. Any half measures in the "whoa" training before proceeding to the pointing exercise will cost the trainer and make his job much more difficult. Only when the dog is completely trained to whoa should he be expected to follow orders when in the presence of game.

Tie both legs of the bird to the end of the string. Have an assistant hold the fishing rod, with the bird resting in short grass. Bring the dog on the long leash so the wind is from the bird to the dog. The handler should be allowing the dog to approach the bird but be holding tightly to the leash. The dog should show signs of scenting the bird and seeing it. If not, the assistant should twitch the rod so the bird flutters. The dog should freeze into a point. The handler commands whoa repeatedly, drawing out the word soothingly and softly while moving hand over hand up the long leash until the handler is up to the dog (pictures 63, 64, 65, 66).

Stroke the dog the whole length of the back and out the underside of the tail while saying wh . . . o . . . a calmly and soothingly. With the right hand holding the leash, place the flattened palm of the left hand under the tail and gently push the dog forward (picture 67). He will resist the pushing, even leaning back into the pressure. Keep repeating wh . . . o . . . a while pushing the dog from the side as well as the rear.

Pictures 63 (above) and 64 (below). While the assistant holds the fishing pole the handler allows the dog to approach the bird, holding tightly to the long leash. When the dog freezes into a point, the handler commands whoa repeatedly and softly while moving hand over hand up the long leash until he is up to the dog. German Wirehaired Pointer. (Photos by Vern Brand).

Pictures 65 (above) and 66 (below). Although the handler keeps a tight hold on the leash as he moves up it, he does not maintain tension on the leash. However, he is ready to hold the dog back with the use of the leash if the dog should attempt to lunge at the bird. Vizsla. (Photos by Vern Brand).

Picture 67. Stroke the dog the whole length of the back and out the underside of the tail while saying wh . . . o . . . a calmly and soothingly. With the right hand holding the leash, place the flattened palm of the left hand under the tail and gently push the dog forward. He will resist the pushing, even leaning back into the pressure. Keep repeating wh . . . o . . . a while pushing the dog from the side as well as the rear. German Shorthaired Pointer. (Photo by Vern Brand).

The handler should now be able to move ahead of the dog without the loss of intensity of the point. If the dog tries to move up, command "whoa" a bit more sharply and hold him back with the leash. Have the assistant flick the rod to move the bird. The dog should remain staunch. The bird can now be lifted upward and away as though taking off. Whoa the dog. The bird should be dropped 10 to 12 feet ahead of the dog.

The dog should not move to chase it. Hold him back with the leash and the "whoa" command. The dog can relax intensity but not leave the spot. When the dog is standing calmly, again lead him up on the bird. When he points, and the handler has repeated the staunching, the assistant can walk in front of the dog, pick up the bird and toss it toward the dog. The dog must stay still. The handler should then pick up the dog, lifting him off point, and carry him away to end the lesson. Never drag or pull the dog from a point, always lift the dog and carry him away.

STEP 2.

The preceding step may be repeated. However, a new location, away from the normal training area should be chosen. The dog should not be given the opportunity to associate birds with his home training area only. The exercise should not be repeated more than once. The purpose of the exercise is just an expansion of "whoa" using sight pointing as an inducement to make the dog move. The "whoa" is reinforced and strengthened, but this time in the presence of game. It must not be overdone. Too much sight pointing and whoaing will make the dog overcautious and can hinder him in handling game later on. It might make him tend to blink game. Blinking is deliberately avoiding game when scenting it.

STEP 3.

The dog can now be taken to the field where he must begin pointing by scent without sighting the game. The most certain way to have the dog find birds is to put the birds there and knowing before hand where the birds are planted. There are many ways of planting birds, the technique and species of bird used will depend on many things such as availability of birds, availability of open areas to work the dog and many others.

Assuming the dog has been exercised in areas where he has found birds and he has shown a good tendency to point but has never been prevented from chasing, the release of quail and a recall cage can be used. If the trainer has only 2 or 3 quail available, these can be used and recovered by tying a brightly colored piece of knitting yarn to one leg of each bird. The piece of yarn should trail about 4 feet behind the bird. This shortens the flight of the bird and if marked down, the handler can easily locate the bird and by grabbing the end of the yarn can recapture it for later use. Commercially available or home made spring-release traps can also be used, but these devices tend to make the situation more complicated for the trainer who has not had experience with them.

Which method of releasing birds is used is not so important. However, releases or plantings of birds should be done wearing gloves to avoid the scent of the handler on the birds. If pheasants are used, they can be dizzied or rocked to sleep and gently placed on their side. Quail should not be dizzied, but tossed tail first into the grass. Dizzied quail sometimes cannot fly for a considerable time afterward and in this lesson, the bird should not flutter about, but should be able to get up and fly away.

Assuming 2 or 3 birds are planted at several locations in a field, the dog can be hunted into the wind, toward where the first bird is located. The long leash should be attached to the collar and the dog dragging it freely. The area chosen for the lessons should be grass and weeds, not brushy or shrubby, so the leash drags easily.

When the dog locates a bird and points, get to the dog quickly, but do not rush suddenly. Pick up the leash and work hand over hand along the leash to the dog as in Step 1. Repeat the drawn out w...h...o...a over and over. Stroke the dog and staunch him as in Step 1. When the dog is calm but still intense, drag up the leash and get a good hold on the end. Keep holding the leash and walk out in front of the dog and flush the bird, all the time keep crooning the "whoa" softly and drawn out. Keep a close eye on the dog so you can anticipate his movement and caution him with a sharper "whoa".

Picture 68. The leash is looped around a post (out of picture on left). The handler maintains the backward pull on the dog who is just beginning to get snubbed up and tumbled over. Pudelpointer. (Photo by Eldon Stonehouse, Toronto Globe and Mail).

Some dogs might not let the handler out in front without charging the bird. In order to overcome this problem, plant a bird a few feet upwind from a solid post. Instead of approaching the dog up the leash, loop the leash around the post so the long leash runs from the dog back around the post and forward again to the handler. This way the handler can maintain a backward pull on the dog and can still walk out in front of him (picture 68).

Despite these preparations, the dog might break and attempt to chase when the bird flushes. If he does, command "whoa" only one time, but very sharply. Haul back on the leash just as the dog reaches the end so the dog is lifted off his feet and falls backwards. Quickly walk to the dog, pick him up and carry him to the exact spot where he was pointing. Stand him there, command "whoa" and move out in front of him. Kick around in the grass and create all sorts of disturbing things to encourage him to break but keep saying "whoa" soothingly and drawn out. The handler might also carry a live bird (especially if using quail) in a pocket of his coat for releasing at this moment or for tossing into the grass to be flushed for immediate reinforcement of the lesson. Return to the dog, carry him 20 to 30 feet away from the spot, set him down facing in a direction other than that taken by the bird when it flew and send him on to hunt another bird. Keep repeating this step in various locations until the dog remains perfectly still when the bird flushes. Any further breaking or chasing should be punished harshly to make the dog understand that this is an absolute no.

If the dog does not chase and remains steady to the flush, praise the dog, carry him from the spot and start him in a new direction. Do not allow the dog to return to the spot where the bird was planted. Allowing repeated returning will encourage pottering. Do not allow the dog to run toward where the bird flew, especially if the bird flew only a short distance. Rather, quickly work the dog toward a second planted bird and repeat the exercise. The dog will soon learn there are more birds to be found and the spot where the first bird had been is an unproductive place once the bird has flown.

The dog that has progressed properly through all the steps of whoa will not present the problem of chasing. But, dogs hurried through the whoa lessons and introduced to free flying game too quickly or incorrectly, or dogs hunted over before being correctly trained, almost certainly will present problems. Also, the dog that has heard "whoa" yelled at him every time he chased, but without the simultaneous control and reinforcement from the handler or before he was properly prepared will be a problem. Proper and complete preparation of the dog before trying to whoa him in the presence of game cannot be emphasized too strongly.

The dog might flush a bird accidently or deliberately during the early stages of this step. If this should happen and the dog breaks and chases before the handler can grab the leash, the handler should not attempt to whoa the dog. Only when the handler is certain he can enforce the "whoa" — that is he is holding the leash — should he give the command. No command should ever be given unless it can be enforced. Once the dog gets away without obeying, he will attempt it everytime. Bad habits form easily and are hard to break.

Step 4.

Having a dog remain still to flush is one thing, having the dog remain standing when a bird is shot out of the air and falls is quite another—especially for dogs that love to retrieve.

When Step 3 has been mastered and assuming the dog has sound nerves and has been exposed to all manner of noises such as hand clapping, hammering, banging pans and so on during the earlier training of "whoa", the dog can be steadied to shot.

Proceed as in Step 3, keeping the dog on the long leash. Begin the shooting with a small bang and proceed through increasing loudness up to the average shot gun sound. A blank .22 cal. is good loudness for starting. After the dog has stood quietly for 15 or 20 seconds after the bird has flushed, the handler can fire the shot. The dog should be watched closely for signs of flinching or cowering. A dropped tail and/or lowered head is an indication the dog is soft on the gun and the handler must proceed differently and with caution or hard to solve problems might be created.

Normally, the shot will only increase the dog's intensity, and not frighten the dog. The shot should be followed with a "whoa" command a bit sharper than the soothing, crooned whoas while the dog pointed and during the flush. Do this step only one or two times during a single session, making sure the dog holds steady each time. The loudness can be increased to louder calibre blanks or to a light shotgun. Each time the shot should be followed quickly by the "whoa". After only a few lessons the dog will associate the shot with whoa and the shot alone will mean stop, do not move.

When certain the dog has no fear of the shooting and the dog is steady, an assistant should be used as the shooter. Preferably, the assistant will be a good shot and will shoot only when told to do so. A bird can now be shot for the dog. But, the shooter must be told not to shoot the flushed bird if the dog does not perform perfectly. The handler should concentrate on his dog, steady and staunch him on point, flush the bird and be sure the dog holds. If the dog is steady to the flush, the gunner should allow the bird to get 25 to 30 yards out in front before firing. The handler ensures the dog is steady and keeps holding the leash. The dog should be made to remain standing for at least 30 seconds or longer if he is very excited. When the dog is calm but concentrating on where the bird fell, the leash can be snapped off and the dog sent to retrieve if all his retrieving training is complete.

The dog can also be required to stand steady while the handler walks out and picks up the bird. If this is done, the handler should show the bird to the dog and not let the dog go to where the bird had dropped. Rather send him away in another direction. The purpose of this is to reinforce to the dog that he must not move until told to do so.

Many hunters will want their dog to break at shot to make the retrieve more quickly. Therefore they will want to skip this step. However, the versatile dog must also be useful in the duck blind and therefore he should not break on every shot. He might, in fact, be required to remain quiet and still through a whole barrage of shooting.

By training the dog to be steady to wing and shot, the versatile hunter with his versatile dog can have his cake and eat it too. Once trained thoroughly to be steady to the shot and the falling bird until told to "fetch", the dog can be easily untrained in the upland shooting and retrained in the waterfowl shooting if desired.

While hunting, the handler will also be the shooter and without trying can untrain his dog. The handler works his dog just as in the lessons up to the point of the shot. He need only give the command "fetch" immediately after shooting a few times and the dog will associate the shot with "fetch", thereby anticipating the command. Most dogs will quickly learn to break on the shot under these circumstances. However, the handler must be able to "whoa" the dog with a single command in case of a miss. A few repetitions of "whoa" with the unharmed bird flying away and not falling and the intelligent dog will quickly learn the difference between a hit and miss.

Some dogs might make a further assocation however, and begin breaking at the flush. This is not desirable and must be curbed immediately. Also, the dog learning to break on the shot can now present a problem in waterfowl shooting, but need not do so. A few reinforcing lessons to remain steady during and after the shot and the dog can quickly learn the difference between the upland shooting and the duck blind shooting.

If the dog has never been steady to shot and has not been trained to be, the handler can expect only chaos in the duck blind. He has no recourse but to start the training at the beginning if he wants a useful dog. Always, it is much easier to let the dog relax or ease off from what he has learned than to have him perform some task he has never learned.

STEP 5.

Many North American hunters prefer having 2 or more dogs working simultaneously when hunting in a group. This social hunting can quickly become a shambles if one or more of the dogs is poorly trained and exhibits bad manners. One dog stealing a point from another or rushing past and flushing the other dog's point shortens tempers of dogs and hunters alike. Worse is two dogs rushing to retrieve one bird. The ensuing disagreement can result in both the bird and the dogs returning in pieces. So, backing or honoring another dog's point and retrieve is desirable.

However, backing is not one of the versatile dogs' long suits. The versatile dog is not the pointing machine only, he is also the retriever. He was designed to be the whole show — before and after the shot. He has a great desire to please his master and he knows with just a little experience that pointing a bird and retrieving it to his master pleases and earns him praise. The normal versatile dog is not going to allow another dog to win the praise if he can help it. The personality of the versatile dog is not suited for sharing the hunt. This generality will not apply to all individuals. Some are born with intense backing ability. The experiences the dog had while growing up also will alter his behavior. The best way to hunt with 2 or more dogs is to have one working while the other (s) are walking at heel. The dogs are each worked in turn, but only one working at any one time. Or, work one while leaving the others in the car or kennel. The dogs can each be given an hour or so of work in turn.

Many people will want their dogs to back and usually this must be taught the versatile dog. First, the dog must be completely steady to wing and shot and must be obedient to "whoa" at any distance and in any circumstance. An assistant and another dog that is also completely steady will be required.

A bird should be planted so it cannot run away or flush wild. The second dog should be on point on the bird. Lead your dog on the long leash up toward the pointing dog but from an angle so the scent of the bird is not coming to him. If your dog indicates a tendency for backing on seeing the other dog on point, you need only caution him with a drawn out wh . . . o . . . a. Move up the leash to the dog and stroke him, calming and staunching him as was done in pointing. The assistant should then move in to staunch the other dog. Flush and shoot the bird. The other dog should make the retrieve. Your dog must be held steady through it all with the leash if necessary. The hardest moment for your dog will be when the other dog makes the retrieve. Praise your dog lavishly for a correct performance. The next bird should be pointed, shot and retrieved for your dog while the other is made to back. Alternating dogs on successive birds will strengthen the obedience in both dogs.

If your dog shows no tendency to back when being led in, but indicates he wants to push right on past, he must be forcibly "whoaed". Whoa your dog 10 to 15 yards from the dog on point. Prevent him from scenting the bird if at all possible. He must learn to point at the sight of another dog on point, not because he smells the bird. Move up to your dog, holding him with repeated drawn out "whoas". Calm him by stroking and pressure from the rear. When the dog is in control of his own temperament, the assistant can flush and shoot. Stand or kneel to the front of your dog so to see his eyes and ears for indications of breaking. Anticipate and "whoa" him more sharply if he attempts to move. If your dog does break and must be hauled up short on the leash, carry him back to the exact spot and make him remain standing until the other dog has completed the retrieve. Again, alternate dogs on successive birds.

As your dog shows increasing tendency toward backing, he is associating the pointing dog with whoaing and when the association is complete, the "whoa" will no longer be required.

Do not attempt to whoa your dog to back another if he is not on the long leash. If he charges in when off the leash, it means he has not yet learned it while on the leash. Yelling whoa at this time would only teach disobedience. The more desire the dog has, the harder it will be to teach backing. Some dogs may never back, others can learn quickly. If the dog shows signs of souring on birds because of the force involved in making him back, do not continue. Allow the dog to regain his enthusiasm before attempting it again.

Another caution is when your dog does back and behaves perfectly even while the other dog retrieves, do not pair him with a dog that is not equally well trained. Your work can be destroyed in a few minutes by the other dog. Dogs do learn by example, particularly bad examples.

Chapter 9

THE DOWN

Picture 69. The correct position for the "down". The dog's head should be flat on the ground between the front legs and the dog should not be allowed to move. Griffons. (Photo by Edward Bailey).

"Down" is the strongest control command. The dog that knows and obeys this command instantly under all circumstances and at any distance is under the control of the handler in any situation. Some handlers feel the "whoa" is adequate and will not resort to the "down". Others might feel insecure with their dog whoaed but still standing, particularly with the strong willed dog. Still others might want the dog to go down flat to the flush, particularly those who use their dogs for hunting rabbits or hares. "Down" is always a sharp command and always demands instant response.

EQUIPMENT REQUIRED:
1. Collar, preferably spiked choker collar.
2. Short leash.
3. Long leash.
4. Whistle.

STEP 1.

The dog must be very well along with "sit" and walking at heel on the leash. The dog is made to sit beside the left foot of the handler. The dog is on the short leash. Drop the leash beside the dog. Place the left hand over the back of the dog's neck and, pressing on the collar, push the dog downward. Simultaneously lift the front legs up and forward with the right hand while giving the command "down" (picture 70).

The dog might attempt to raise his back end. Prevent this by pressing down on the kidney region with the left hand and holding the head down with the right hand. Hold the dog in this position for about 30 to 40 seconds with

Picture 70. *Place the left hand over the back of the dog's neck and, pressing on the collar, push the dog downward. Simultaneously lift the front legs up and forward with the right hand, give the command "down". Griffon. (Photo by Edward Bailey).*

Picture 71. *Prevent the dog from raising his back end by pressing down on the kidney region with the left hand and holding the head down with the right hand. Hold the dog in the "down" position for 30 to 40 seconds with very slight praise. Griffon. (Photo by Edward Bailey).*

Picture 72. *After the dog no longer attempts to lift his head or get up, slowly lift both hands away from the dog. If the dog attempts to lift his head or get up, immediately command "down" and quickly press the dog down again. Griffon. (Photo by Edward Bailey).*

Picture 73.
Once the trainer can stand erect over the dog for up to one minute, the dog can be commanded more harshly when he raises his head. Griffon.
(Photo by Edward Bailey).

Picture 74.
The dog must learn to remain in the "down" position even when the handler is out of sight. Stand behind the dog so that he cannot see you. If the dog raises his head, give a harsh command. Repeat the exercise until the dog's behavior is dependable. Griffon.
(Photo by Edward Bailey).

Picture 75. The handler should now be able to walk all around the dog, walk over him, etc., without the dog raising his head. Griffon. (Photo by Edward Bailey).

very slight praising (picture 71). The dog's head should be flat on the ground between the front legs and the dog should not be allowed to move during this time. Repeat "down" with every correction, no matter how slight. The dog must learn that no punishment or pressure is applied as long as he remains in the down position.

When the dog has been held in the down position for a short period, the handler stands erect and commands "come", allowing the dog to stand up and walk with the handler.

STEP 2.

After Step 1 has been repeated sufficiently so the dog no longer attempts to raise his head or roll over or get up, slowly lift both hands away from the dog (picture 72). But, if the dog attempts to lift his head or get up, immediately command "down" and quickly press the dog down again. Keep repeating until the dog lies quietly in position with the hands lifted completely away and the handler can stand upright.

Each lesson is terminated with the command "come" and the dog is led away walking at heel. Praise of the dog should be slight. This sequence is the one time in all the training when praise should not be overdone.

Gradually the handler will be able to stand over the dog for up to a minute. When the handler can stand over the dog (Picture 72) and behind the dog (Picture 73) for a period of time without corrections, the lesson has been learned.

STEP 3.

The dog must now learn to go "down" on command without being placed in the position. To accomplish this, the dog is first sitting beside the handler. The leash runs from the dog's collar under the handler's left foot and the end is held snuggly by the left hand. With the command "down" the handler raises his right arm vertically as a visual signal to the dog. At the same time a sharp upward tug on the leash pulls the dog toward the ground. The dog must begin learning to go down quickly on the command.

Be very sure the dog is positioned correctly. The dog should lie straight on both his hind legs, the front legs should be stretched forward and parallel and the head should lie flat on the ground between the two front legs. These details are important because the dog is in a completely subordinate posture and knows it. Especially, be sure the head is flat on the ground and not raised in the slightest

When the dog has learned to go down on the voice and raised arm signals and no longer needs to be tugged down, the whistle command can be introduced. To do this, drop out the voice command "down" and substitute one long blast on the whistle when the arm is raised. The dog will quickly make the association between whistle and raised arm and now has three commands — voice, arm and whistle — all meaning "down". The commands can all be used interchangeably.

STEP 4.

The handler must now attempt to keep the dog down when out of sight of the dog. First the handler moves to the front of the dog, always keeping in the dog's field of vision (Picture 74). Then the handler moves to the left side and around in front to the right side. Finally the handler moves around behind the dog. If the dog turns his head give a command until the behavior is dependable.

Gradually the distance from the dog can be increased, the handler can walk around the dog, jump over the dog (picture 75), or have an assistant cause some disturbance such as calling, throwing objects past the dog and so on. The dog is still kept on leash but the distance can be increased now by changing to the long leash. Each time the dog makes any effort to get up or raise his head, a sharp tug and the command "down" is used to replace the dog in the proper position. The dog should learn to lie in the down position for at least five minutes, unconcerned, whether the handler is in view or not and without being influenced by disturbances.

STEP 5.

The dog must now learn to go down from a standing position and while moving. If the dog has thoroughly mastered steps 1 through 4 the dog can be commanded "down" from the standing position in the same fashion as from the sitting position (picture 77). Then proceed to the "down" while the dog is walking, then running at various speeds. This is accomplished while having the dog walk or trot at heel on the short leash. Suddenly blow the "down" command on the whistle but the handler keeps moving. A sharp downward tug on the leash might be necessary to reinforce the whistle command. Do not allow any hesitation in the dog. Usually there is no difficulty in this step.

STEP 6.

When the dog will go down quickly on command—voice, whistle and hand signal and is also responding immediately and cheerfully to the "come" command, then lessons to teach the dog to obey "down" at a distance can begin. The dog can be either sitting, standing or walking in an enclosed yard and on the long leash. The dog should be 2 to 5 yards away from the handler. At a moment when the dog is not expecting a command to go down, command "down" by lifting the arm vertically and add either the verbal or whistle

Picture 76. *The handler should now be able to cause other distractions, without the dog raising his head. Griffon. (Photo by Edward Bailey)*

Picture 77. *The dog must now learn to go down from a standing position and while moving. He should be responding to voice, whistle, or hand signal. Griffon. (Photo by Edward Bailey).*

command. Usually the dog will obey quickly if he has been properly prepared. If the dog hesitates or walks a few steps while going down, jerk on the leash. Be sure the dog goes into the correct drop position with his chain flat on the ground.

Gradually increase the distance to the whole length of the leash. Also, practice outside the yard, and introduce distractions. Create many new situations, the more the better, especially when the dog is not expecting to be given the "down" command. An assistant can run with the dog on the long leash while the handler stays at some distance and whistles the "down". The assistant must immediately correct the dog if he hesitates or does not go into the proper down position.

Always watch for the correct and prompt execution of the command "down". Any carelessness by the dog should be punished hard, but praise should be given when the dog does well. The dog must understand that the "down" does not mean unpleasantness for him when he obeys quickly and correctly. When the dog understands this completely, all future exercises will go quite easily. The handler can then proceed to work with the dog off the leash, first in an enclosed yard, then outside the yard and with distractions.

Do not hurry through these exercises. Each step must be mastered completely before proceeding to the next step. Finally, work the dog in the fields and woods until the dog obeys "down" quickly at distances up to 150 yards. The most important thing to remember is that the dog must obey "down" every time and quickly. Slackness or hesitation should not be tolerated under any condition.

Chapter 10

FLUSHING ON COMMAND

Many times in the course of normal hunting a pointing dog locates game and points in an inaccessible place or in a place where the hunter cannot get a shot if he must do the flushing himself. In these situations the well trained dog can be given a command to flush the birds when the trainer has located himself in the best possible position. Many intelligent dogs will learn this by themselves by experience, others with an extremely strong pointing instinct will not learn it even given the proper instruction. However, most versatile dogs can be taught to flush on command fairly easily.

EQUIPMENT REQUIRED:

1. Live birds for planting.
2. Long leash.
3. Small, dense thicket or brush such as a briar patch.

STEP 1.

Before attempting to teach the dog to flush on command, the dog must be well schooled in "whoa" and should be steady to flush and shot. Particularly, do not attempt this until the dog is responding to "whoa" flawlessly in the presence of flushing game. This means that the dog is quite experienced and in many cases has reached 2 to 3 years of age.

Plant a bird, quail or pigeon preferably, in field cover. Allow the dog to find and point it. Go up to the dog and when beside the dog, command in an excited voice "get it up" and urge the dog forward. A tap on the back of the head might be necessary to urge the dog on. Keep repeating "get it up" excitedly until the dog moves in and flushes the bird. Be ready to "whoa" the dog as soon as the bird flushes. Then praise the dog well and head him out in a direction different from that taken by the bird.

The lesson can be repeated the same way and the bird may be shot. Be sure the dog has whoaed before shooting, however. Wait a short interval and command "fetch". Do not allow the dog to anticipate the command to flush the bird. If the dog should start to move before the command, stop him quickly with a stern "whoa".

STEP 2.

When the dog is responding well by flushing quickly on command in the field, move to an area where there is a small thicket, bramble patch or similar thick, impenetrable cover. Pull the primary feathers from one wing of a quail or chukkar partridge and release the bird into the thicket. Bring the dog up to the thicket. Command "get it up". Whether the dog scents the bird and points or does not point is of no importance. The important thing is the dog knows he is released from pointing and is to flush whatever is in the thicket.

Let the dog chase the bird around in the thicket and when the bird runs out, shoot it on the ground ahead of the dog if possible. Simultaneously "whoa" the dog, then send him to retrieve the bird.

From this point on, the dog should understand he is to point when possible and flush only on command. The command "get it up" can come after an established point and from various distances or it can come before a point is established and means go in, search and flush it out, bypassing the pointing. However, care must be taken to insure the dog does not flush before the command to do so.

The handler must have absolute control over the dog before attempting these exercises. Perfect response to the "whoa" command is necessary for this control.

Chapter 11

CARE OF THE VERSATILE HUNTING DOG

Feeding and Housing the Dog

Feeding should present no problems for dog or master. Most modern commercially available dry dog foods are completely adequate diets for the dog. Both the Gaines Research Laboratories and the Ralston Purina Research Laboratories have published material available on the feeding of dogs. The only caution is that the recommended diets are maintenance diets primarily. The dog that is working hard requires more energy intake than the dog that is not working hard. Also, individual dogs differ in their rates of metabolism of energy and food must be adjusted according to individual requirements.

Housing has not been as well researched as feeding. Many myths persist such as the erroneous belief that a hunting dog should not live in the master's house and many others.

The versatile hunting dog was developed to live in or at the home of his master. However, the dog that lives in the master's house should have his own place where he is fed, watered and bedded. The dog's place should be decided upon and then used consistently. Food should be given at the same place every day, not just anywhere. Water should be available at the same place all the time. The dog's bed should be in a cool, comfortable location and that is where the dog should sleep always. The dog should never be allowed to simply shift for himself.

The dog should not have his bed close to any heat source, such as a radiator or furnace. The bed should also not be in a damp or wet location. Do not have the dog housed in an active horse or cattle stable. The concentrated ammonia from urine is detrimental to the dog's nose. Always avoid keeping the dog in a room where there is a strong odor of oil, gasoline and exhaust fumes or any other strong oil based odors.

After these cautions have been taken into consideration, the master's house is perfectly suitable for the hunting dog and in most cases is the best environment for the dog. The close contact between dog and master is necessary for the versatile hunting dog. This close contact is easiest to maintain if the dog is living with the master. Obviously, disobedience in the house should not be tolerated any more than it should be tolerated outside the house. The well trained versatile hunting dog is capable of being an excellent pet, watchdog and hunting companion.

The dog can have a kennel outside with an enclosed run. The kennel should be cool and shaded in summer, warm and protected from wind in winter and should be dry and clean. The floor of the run can be cement, gravel, sand or black top. Black top paving must be washed thoroughly before putting a dog on it. Oil and creosote burn the feet of a dog.

The kennel is essential to the person who has several dogs. However, the kennel should not be just a storage space for dogs when they are not being used for hunting. The dog living in a kennel should be given as much attention as the dog living in the home. Do not ignore the dog simply because he is out of his master's house. Special effort must be made to give the dog as much contact with his handler as possible, especially while the dog is young.

Grooming the Dog

The grooming of a versatile hunting dog is not meant to imply the niceties of the show ring. Primarily, grooming a hunting dog is for the dog's own comfort.

Care of the dog's coat is no problem in the shorthaired breeds. The wirehaired breeds present the biggest problems of coat care and the long haired breeds are intermediate. Shorthaired dogs require only occasional brushing to remove dead hair. Long haired breeds might show some matting or tangling but can be kept well groomed with frequent brushing and combing.

The coats of the wirehaired group can vary from short hard hair to long soft curly hair as well as hair of proper length and consistency. Many wirehaired dogs need frequent stripping or plucking. Stripping is done with a specially constructed stripping comb either with or without a blade. Plucking is pulling out the dead hair by using the thumbs and forefingers to pluck the hair with the grain, that is pluck in the direction in which the hair lies. The dead, loose hair will pull out easily and the live healthy hair will remain.

Many individuals of the wirehaired breeds require periodic clipping to keep the coat manageable, especially those individuals with soft and/or long hair. The face and head areas particularly require clipping or trimming. A great excess of hair is as detrimental to the dog as a sparce, open coat.

Care of the ears is another absolute must in most versatile hunting dogs. Those dogs that have a lot of hair in the external ear canal present the worst problem. Because the ears hang down on the versatile dogs, the ear canals stay warm and moist, presenting prime growing conditions for yeasts, fungi and bacteria. A growth of hair in the ear canal increases the chances of infection.

The ears should be washed out with a mild peroxide solution or an antiseptic solution obtainable from a veterinarian. The ear canals should be plucked free of hair and kept dry by applications of coarse powder. Indications of ear infections are shaking the head and scratching the ears. Yeast infections are most common and most difficult to cure. Yeast can be diagnosed by a sour smell from the ear and a dark brown waxy deposit in the ear canal. Yeast infections cause itching in the ear and a secondary bacterial infection can arise from the dog scratching. Keeping the ears clean and dry is the best cure for yeast infections.

Toenails should be kept short. Nails that are too long tend to split and can incapacitate a dog for an entire hunting season. Extremely long, untended toenails also act to change the dog's stance and way of running, resulting eventually in crippling the dog. The toenails should be cut once each week or two, or less frequently if the dog is walking or running on an abrasive surface such as cement.

In the Field While Hunting

Perhaps it should go without saying that the most important hunting companion is the dog and he should be treated accordingly. His eyes, feet, coat, mouth and nose must be tended to if he is to keep in top hunting condition. After each trip to the field the dog's eyes should be checked for weed and grass seeds, particularly under the lower eyelid. The eyes should be bathed with a tear drop solution obtained from a veterinarian.

Similarly feet should be checked after each day afield. Sharp pointed grass seeds and ground growing thistles, thorns and burrs tend to lodge between toes and cause infection if not removed. The dog should be checked, over his entire body, for burrs, but especially in the areas under the legs. Keep the coat as free from irritants as possible.

During hot, dry conditions, a wet cloth should be carried in a plastic bag. Wipe the dog's mouth and nose frequently, both to keep him cool and to moisten his nose and mouth. Another kindness to a dog, particularly during hot weather is to clean the loose feathers or fur from his mouth after he has retrieved shot game.

Feeding a dog properly during the periods of hard work is essential. The dog may be fed very lightly before hunting but save the heavy feeding until the end of the day. Extra protein should be added either by feeding high protein diet or adding red meat to his regular food. The amount of food given should be increased to compensate for the energy burned during the hunt. Either pieces of meat or sugar in the form of lump sugar, cookies, candy or better still, corn syrup should be given to the dog once each hour while hunting. The dog is burning up energy rapidly and must replenish it in an easily utilized form or the dog can suffer severely from low blood sugar (hypoglycemia).

If no water is available where the dog is being hunted, water should be provided for the dog. Water can be carried in a large thermos jug in the car or if not able to return to the car frequently, a canteen of water should be carried along.

Traveling Precautions

Most dogs can travel well enough by car. Some dogs suffer cronically from car sickness but this is not overly common. The best way of transporting a dog in a car of any kind is inside a dog crate. Crates are commercially available or can be built by the handyman. If a dog is to be transported in a station wagon but not in a dog crate, a barrier of some sort separating the cargo space where the dog will be from the rear seat is safest for the dog as well as other passengers and the driver.

Carrying a dog in the trunk of a normal sedan is not a good practice. Exhaust fumes can accumulate, air circulation and cooling is minimal. Also, oxygen might be limited.

A well trained dog can be made to curl up on the floor on the passenger's side and remain quietly for hours. This provides a good safe carrying place for the dog. The rear seat is also a good place to carry the dog, particularly if there is an adequate barrier separating the front from the rear seats. The barrier is primarily to protect the dog, driver and passengers in case of a sudden stop.

Transportation by air is best done when the dog is accompanying the handler on the same flight. The dog should be suitably crated and shipped in the cargo compartment. A very good practice is to inform the airlines in no uncertain terms that you have the dog travelling with you and fully expect him to arrive as safely and as surely as any other paying passenger on the flight. Also be certain the dog is transferred correctly if any transfering is necessary. If available, a through and non-stop flight is the best.

FIRST AID

A very simple first aid kit should be carried whenever you take the dog afield:

1. Hemostat (quills, bloodvessels, ears)
2. Shoestring (muzzle, tourniquet)
3. Corn syrup
4. Gauze 3" wide
5. Elastic tape

Depending on the temperature, the location of the terrain, the availability of water and the temperament of the dog, heat prostration can spoil not only a day's hunt but often endanger the wellbeing of a good dog for some time. To avoid this malady, first of all, have a well exercised dog. Dogs that are kept in the kennel all year and turned loose the first day of hunting are much more prone to be affected by heat prostration than a physically well prepared dog.

Before the season starts the dog should be exercised regularly especially in the morning or evening while it is cool. Also long swims in the water are helpful to build the dog up. A wingclipped duck released in a good sized pond will keep most dogs busy for a good time even during the heat of the day. For land exercise in the morning or evening, roading in a harness beside car or bicycle is excellent, as long as it is done slow and not more than 20 minutes to begin with. While roading, the dog sets the pace by pulling.

In case a day's hunt is planned in warm weather the owner is well advised to carry with him *corn syrup* or honey in a plastic squeeze bottle and every 30 minutes about one teaspoon is dispensed directly into the dog's mouth. This will help to keep the blood sugar at a normal level.

Should a dog suffer from heat prostration he should be kept as cool as possible and rushed to a veterinarian.

Hyperventilation is another form of overwork, especially during hot weather, which can cause serious side effects. Dogs inhale too much oxygen while puffing hard after hard work. They usually start to stagger and lose balance, appearing to be drunk. They should be cooled down as fast as possible by submerging the body in water, and should be kept walking on a leash in a shaded place until recovered. But again, a physically well prepared dog will not be affected as easily.

A *hemostat* is one of the most versatile instruments for first aid in case of hard bleeding from a cut or when the dog has an encounter with a porcupine. A profoundly bleeding blood vessel can be clamped shut with the hemostat until a vet can be found. Also all porcupine quills that large pliers cannot reach can be pulled.

A *shoestring* about 24" will serve as a muzzle to tie a dog's mouth while he is in pain during first aid. It also can be used as a tourniquet to cut off bleeding on the extremeties.

A roll of *elastic tape* and *gauze* completes a first aid kit for emergencies in the field. But, whenever on a hunting trip with your dog, a good precaution to follow is to know beforehand the location of the nearest Veterinarian. First aid, at best, is only a stop-gap measure until proper care can be obtained. However, common sense and first aid can save your dog's life.

Chapter 12

TWELVE GOLDEN RULES FOR TRAINING

1. Talk with a low voice. Only when your dog is disobedient on a task he has been taught correctly, should you raise your voice.

2. Be consistent and insistent. Let your dog know during training that you are the team boss.

3. Do not end a lesson with negative results, or an uncooperative dog.

4. Take every opportunity at home and afield to teach the young dog self control. If you keep him in the house he should be confined to his place several times a day and learn to stay there quietly.

5. When you are outside, busy with something other than your dog, put him on the leash or, if he has been taught, make him stay on a spot. Never permit the young dog to wander around and look for his own excitement or exercise.

6. Wherever there is traffic; cars, trains, etc., keep your dog on the leash. Even the best trained dog can be tempted to cross the street.

7. Always be ready with praise when your dog cooperates and share with him the good feeling that results from cooperative teamwork.

8. If misbehavior calls for punishment, do not be lukewarm — be hot, but do not punish in rage or temper.

9. After punishment, do not put the dog in his kennel immediately and walk away mad. Make him do what he was supposed to do, praise him and then put him in the kennel. Always put the dog on a leash before you punish him.

10. If your dog does not want to come to you, do not chase him. Walk away in the opposite direction and, if necessary, hide. Never punish your dog when he finally decides to come to you.

11. Once your young dog's natural abilities such as pointing, love for game finding, and use of nose are established, his contact with game should cease until he can be controlled through training.

12. Do not spend your time on a dog that shows signs of shyness or lack of desire to work. Such dogs will let you down when the going is rough no matter how much training they have received.

ABOUT THE AUTHORS

The authors have donated their time and talent in writing this book on behalf of the versatile hunting dog. They will receive no monetary compensation.
Their reward will be the thanks of versatile hunting dog enthusiasts.

All profits from the sale of the book go to The North American Versatile Hunting Dog Association.

Author Bodo Winterhelt working with one of his young Pudelpointers on the first steps of "whoa", during a Training Clinic. (Photo by Edward Bailey).

Author Ed Bailey works with a young Griffon on the Training table teaching him the "whoa" at a training clinic. (Photo by Vern Brand).

THE AUTHORS

Sigbot "Bodo" Winterhelt has been connected with versatile hunting dogs since boyhood. He handled his first dog successfully in a full Utility Field Trial in Germany when he was 14 years old and ever since has been actively involved in the versatile hunting dog movement. He has owned, trained or handled most of the recognized versatile breeds. Since coming to Canada 20 years ago he has devoted his time to establishing field trials for the versatile breeds in North America and to educating hunters to understand the true potentials of these breeds. His work became the foundation for the Field Trial Standards of The North American Versatile Hunting Dog Association. For over 25 years he has bred and trained Pudelpointers and he was the first to bring this breed to North American. Mr. Winterhelt is a professional trainer and Past President of the North American Versatile Hunting Dog Association. He currently resides in Brandon, Oregon.

Dr. Edward D Bailey is a native of Pennsylvania. He earned the Bachelors and Masters Degrees in Wildlife from the University of Montana and the Doctors Degree from Pennsylvania State University in Animal Behavior. He is presently Professor of Animal Behavior at the University of Guelph in Ontario, Canada. He has worked with and hunted over dogs most of his life and with versatile dogs for the past 10 years. His perspective of dogs is both from the viewpoint of a hunter and a behaviorist. Dr. Bailey has served as Secretary and Director of Judge Development for the North American Versatile Hunting Dog Association. He currently resides in Canada.

NAVHDA
Information & Services

Programs
- Handler Clinics
- Apprentice Judging
- NAVHDA Tests

Test Information Service
- Test Reports
- Dog Reports
- Breeder Reports

NAVHDA Registry
- Dog Registration
- Litter Registration
- Kennel Registration

Membership Services
- Chapter Membership
- International Magazine
- Breeder Support Programs

International Brochures
International Membership Application

For information on these programs and services visit us on the Web at www.navhda.org or contact us at:

NAVHDA
P.O. Box 520
Arlington Hts, IL 60006-0520

Tel: 847/253-6488
Fax: 847/255-5987